NEVER ENOUGH

NEVER ENOUGH

One Lawyer's True Story of How He Gambled His Career Away

MICHAEL J. BURKE

Cover design by ABA Publishing

Printed in the United States of America.

19 18   8 7

Library of Congress Cataloging-in-Publication Data

Burke, Michael, 1946–
    Never enough / by Michael Burke.
        p.   cm.
    Includes index.
    ISBN-13: 978-1-59031-991-8
    ISBN-10: 1-59031-991-5
  1. Burke, Michael, 1946– 2. Gamblers—United States—Biography.
3. Alcoholics—United States—Biography. 4. Lawyers—Alcohol use—United States. 5. Gambling—United States. 6. Alcoholics—Rehabilitation—United States. 7. Compulsive gamblers—Rehabilitation—United States. I. Title.

    HV6710.3.B87A3   2008
    616.89—dc22
    [B]   2008018666

Without Jane, my wife of forty years, I would not have become an attorney nor had the opportunity to enjoy the practice I so loved. I would not have known my daughters, Amy Elizabeth and Kathryn Jane, the joys of my life. I probably would not be alive today.

Through the years of alcoholism, which she came to understand and help me overcome; through parenthood, during which we raised two incredible daughters; and even through a three-year prison term, Jane has been—and continues to be—my rock, my inspiration, my security. Her presence is on every page of this book.

Special acknowledgment to Elizabeth Berriman—

My editor, my sister-in-law, my daughters' aunt, my friend of forty-five years, and one of my victims.
Without you, there would not have been a "Never Enough."

Contents

Alcoholism

1

Victim Quote:
"I've known Mike and his family for fifteen years. Our daughters are good friends. We have common friends in this courtroom right now, and it really pains me. I'm sure his family feels the same devastation my family has felt. But . . . when I look at Mike I don't see him as a victim of gambling addiction. I see him as a cold, calculating criminal."

I was sitting in front of my favorite $100 slot machine. Outside the casino, it was a dreary winter's day. Weeks had passed since there had been a glimmer of sunlight. The feeling of depression was palpable.

Inside the casino, the VIP slot area was bright and alive with the promise of hope and a chance for redemption. The room glowed with colorful lights, and the clanging of bells rang out with the possibility of future jackpots for all who played. Players sat at different machines with their good luck charms in full display—from a rabbit's foot to a picture of a grandchild. The extremely pious taped religious relics to their favorite one-armed bandits. A simple pull of the lever created an opportunity to win back all money lost. As long as the player had tokens, the player had hope.

Only one carrousel offered $100 slot machines and there were five machines on that carrousel. I had hit jackpots on three of them and was playing a fourth while waiting to be paid my $120,000.

Hitting each jackpot only kindled my craving for more. While waiting for the payout, I put in two tokens at a time, pulling the

*lever as fast as I could. A casino host who knew me well ap-
proached from behind. He knew that I had been losing heavily for
months and wanted to encourage me to win even more on this day.
He leaned over and whispered in my ear, "Remember, Burke, it's
never enough." He had uttered the single greatest truth faced by
all addicts.*

*For the second time in my life, an addiction threatened to take
away everything that was dear to me. The first was twenty-five
years ago. How could this all be happening again?*

I come from a long line of distinguished attorneys. My grandfather, George Burke Sr., was a partner in the Burke Law Firm, the
oldest active law firm in Ann Arbor, Michigan. Following the Second World War, he received an appointment as judge at the
Nuremberg Trials, where he heard numerous cases involving Ger-
man war criminals. After the trials concluded, he returned to the
United States with significant political clout.

My father was the second oldest of five children, the one des-
tined to carry on the family legal tradition. After completing his
undergraduate studies at the University of Michigan, he attended
law school at the University of Detroit, after which he joined his
father's firm. Dad soon discovered that he did not enjoy general
practice, so my grandfather used some of his political clout to assist Dad in finding a new job. He contacted the governor of Michigan, G. Mennen "Soapy" Williams, and asked if there were any
positions in state government that would be suitable for my father.
As a result of that meeting, my father received a lifetime appointment, serving as the head of the Michigan Liquor Control Commission. The new job meant that our family would have to relo-
cate, so we moved from Ann Arbor, finally ending up in the small
community of Howell. It was there that my nine brothers and sisters
and I were raised.

Thanks in part to our Irish Catholic background and my father's position with the state, drinking in our home was part of our

lifestyle. In fact, it was not just condoned but actively promoted as part of our family heritage. However, we were regularly warned that it was unacceptable to be involved in any drinking behavior that might cause embarrassment for our father. Fortunately, this was not a problem for me because I had been born with an exceptionally high tolerance, which meant I could drink large quantities of alcohol and not appear intoxicated. Yet, from the very first time I drank, my drinking was different from that of others; I did not especially care for the taste, but I loved the effect it had on me.

At Hillsdale College, my time was equally divided between playing football and drinking. No drinking was allowed during the football season, and anyone caught violating the rule would lose his scholarship, so I never drank during the season. The rest of the year, however, was a different story. I drank a lot, but due to my high tolerance, most of my buddies never knew exactly how much I was drinking. They did know, however, that I was a good friend to have around—the one who would make sure they got home safely after a night of partying. Alcohol worked extremely well for me in my college years.

On August 2, 1968, I married Jane, my high school sweetheart, who was a senior at the University of Michigan. Her father was an attorney in Howell who had been practicing for over fifty years. In 1973, he saw some articles on a new law school opening in Lansing and requested all the necessary material needed to file an application for admission. He was so excited about the possibility of me attending law school that he offered to pay all my expenses. It was the opportunity of a lifetime, and we were ecstatic. It made good sense to both of us that I would become a lawyer and carry on the family tradition.

Those who lack the desire or ability to survive that first year of law school are quickly weeded out. The amount of work is overwhelming, and I realized that all of my time would have to be devoted to studies if I was going to succeed. My fear was that if I continued to drink in my normal manner, I probably would not make it through the first year, so I decided to quit. As it turned out, abstaining from alcohol was not as difficult as I had feared. I was so busy that I hardly missed it. Eventually, I successfully completed the year and was pretty much assured of obtaining a law degree. In my second year of law school, I resumed drinking, but my patterns changed as well as the amount I consumed. I found myself stopping at the bar *every night*.

Despite my growing dependence on alcohol, I graduated from law school. The day of my swearing-in ceremony was one of the best of my life, with family and friends in attendance. Some of my colleagues and family members spoke. I was overwhelmed by a sense of history and family heritage as I took the Lawyers' Oath, one I would eventually betray.

I loved being a general practitioner, and the practice of law was exhilarating. Each day meant new things to learn and new challenges to overcome. I loved the contact with clients and other attorneys, and nothing was more exciting than being involved in settlement negotiations or resolutions of disputes on behalf of my clients. A small general practice is never boring because you have no idea what type of case is coming through the door next.

As my practice began to grow, I was aware that alcohol was taking a more dominant role in my life. I still was unable to admit I had a drinking problem, but for the second time, I made a decision to give it up. This time, in an effort to make my decision irrevocable, I told my friends and family I was going to stop drinking. However, I could not keep this promise because I had become physically addicted. My only option was to lie.

From that point on, I felt forced to be a "closet drinker" and found I was able to survive the day on one pint of vodka. As long as I had access to my pint, I could meet with clients, go to court, and navigate from one end of the day to the other. Alcohol became my daily medication, taken in secret, with my alcoholic symptoms still not visible to family, friends, or associates.

This solution seemed to work for quite a while, but then, one frigid January morning, I had to go to court to finalize a divorce.

The parties had agreed in advance to all the terms, and all I had to do was place their agreement on the record. In legal jargon, lawyers call this "putting on the proofs." After arriving at the courthouse, I decided not to have a drink before going inside. I felt confident I could handle this situation without the assistance of alcohol—but I was wrong. Upon entering the courtroom, my client took the stand to be sworn. All I had to do was ask her a few questions and present the judge with a written judgment. However, I couldn't do it. My hands were shaking, I was sweating profusely, and I couldn't get the words out. The judge saw I was having problems, so he put the proofs on for me and granted my client a judgment of divorce. After the hearing was over, I went back into the judge's chambers. As I tried to apologize for what had happened in court, the judge told me not to worry about it. He had seen young attorneys suffer stage fright many times, and it was nothing to be concerned about; he was confident that it would never happen again.

When I returned to my car, I leaned over, reached under the passenger seat, and grabbed my pint of Gordon's vodka. The pint was ice-cold from the frigid weather. I can still recall the wonderful feeling as I raised it to my lips and took a swallow. It burned as it ran down my throat, but it was a wonderful burn. As I sat in the car, I made a promise to myself that I would never allow this to happen again. I swore I would never again go to court without having a drink first. Alcohol was now interfering with my ability to perform as an attorney.

I knew that if I purchased alcohol at the same store every day some people might start to believe I had a drinking problem. To make sure this did not happen, I found nine or ten different party stores where I could make my purchase. On my way to court one morning, I stopped to get a bottle. As I entered the store, there were three women standing in line waiting to purchase groceries, so I started to walk past them to take my place at the end of the line. The clerk recognized me and immediately stopped what he had been doing and pulled a pint of vodka off the wall. He then put it in a brown paper bag and handed it between two of the women to me. I took the bottle in my left hand and just happened to have the $2.80 in my right hand, the exact cost for the pint of vodka. I was totally humiliated. As I got in my car and drove away, I told myself I would never again purchase anything at that store. Still, by the end of that week, I was back buying another pint.

Shortly after that episode, I experienced the alcoholic's worst nightmare—my tolerance suddenly decreased. I now was getting drunk on the same pint of vodka that used to help get me through the day. Problems started arising at home as well as at work due to my blackouts and other physical symptoms. A dull, aching depression entered my life, and the only release from that pain came when I was drinking.

I decided I needed to make a geographic change and start my life over. One morning after my wife left the house to go to work, I drove to my office and prepared a quitclaim deed transferring ownership of our home to her. I returned to the house and left her a note saying I was leaving. I took $2,500 out of our joint savings account and decided to move to Las Vegas, Nevada. I wanted to be in a place where I could have a good time again.

The last memories I have of that morning were packing my suitcase and leaving the house. Everything that happened in the following twenty-four–hour period was erased from my memory because of an alcohol-induced blackout. The next thing I recall was waking up the following day in McCarran Airport in Las Vegas. I was sitting between two police officers, trying to explain how I had been robbed of all my money. I told them that when I arrived, my intention was to walk from the airport to the casinos, but on the way I was robbed at gunpoint by two men. One of the officers said that he did not believe me; in all the years he had worked in Vegas he had never heard of anyone walking *from* the airport *to* the casinos. Visitors always take a bus, taxi, or limousine to travel the five miles. However, he stated that he was aware that some unlucky visitors had to walk from the casinos back to the airport.

I told them I didn't want to argue anymore; I only wanted to call my wife and ask her to wire me a ticket to fly home.

The flight back to Detroit was one of the longest trips of my life. I had no cash, so I couldn't buy any alcohol, I hadn't bathed in two days, and I was starting to go through withdrawal. When I arrived in Detroit, I was met by two attorney friends who came to drive me home. Neither one of them talked to me on the one-hour drive from the airport. I stared at the backs of their heads, wondering what awaited me when we arrived at the house.

Once I arrived home, my wife calmly explained to me that if I wanted to continue in the marriage, I would have to enter an inpatient rehabilitation program and deal with my problem. By this time we had been happily married for nine years, the only real problems occurring in the past few months as a result of my drinking. I told her I did not want the marriage to end and agreed to seek help.

In April 1977, following my aborted trip, I entered Brighton Hospital, where I was forced to meet my demons. It was the best-known facility in Michigan for dealing with alcohol abuse. It offered a thirty-day inpatient program, with medical support, group therapy, and lectures. There, I was able to survive the physical effects of withdrawal, and thanks to the counseling, I was able to accept the fact that I am an alcoholic. One of my favorite lectures was presented by Dr. Russell Smith, a world-renowned speaker on alcoholism. He talked to us about the dangers of cross-addiction and how we must guard against trading an addiction to alcohol for some other addiction after we left treatment. He warned us: "If you can smoke it, inject it, snort it, swallow it, or roll it [dice in gambling], you are the people who can become addicted to it." This lecture, like most of the talks I heard at Brighton Hospital, made perfect sense at the time.

My life turned around due in large part to Brighton Hospital. Within a year after I finished the program, our first child was born, and we were a family. Five years later, our second child was born, and she made us the perfect family. Our daughters were raised in a house of love. Everything about raising them was fun, and every day with them was better than the day before.

In the following years, I became involved in many community-based activities. I felt a responsibility to give back to the community that had been so good to me. I was on the boards of the county United Way and the ARC (formerly known as the Association for Retarded Citizens) as well as the Livingston County Counseling Board. I was a founder of Howell Public Schools Citizens Advisory Committee, and the cochair of three Howell Public School millage campaigns.

Shortly after completing the Brighton Hospital program, I made the decision to leave the firm I had been with and become a sole practitioner. My practice became one of the best in the county. My client base was comprised mostly of alcoholics or the families of alcoholics. I learned important lessons from these people: Alcoholics always must have traumatic events going on in their lives. The traumas create "smoke," and people close to the alcoholic watch that and fail to look at the person. These clients came to me seeking representation, and I would immediately send them to obtain help for their problems.

I sent so many people to Brighton Hospital over the years that they put me on their board of directors. My clients would enter the inpatient program, learn how to deal with their addiction, resolve their legal problems, and in many instances reclaim their lives. Thanks to the program at Brighton Hospital, my own life was almost perfect—except for one thing. Because I had not paid close enough attention to the advice of Dr. Smith against trading one addiction for another, I ended up celebrating my twenty-fourth, twenty-fifth, and twenty-sixth years of sobriety in Jackson Prison. I am a compulsive gambler.

Gambling 2

Victim Quote:
"... and he knew exactly what he was doing.
He didn't steal for one day, one month. He embezzled
for years."

At the time I completed the program at Brighton Hospital in 1977, there was very little legal gambling in the state of Michigan. About the only thing available was the lottery and I had absolutely no interest in that, so Dr. Smith's warnings about gambling seemed to have little impact on my life. However, looking back, I can see that the seeds of the compulsive gambling addiction were planted shortly after my release from treatment.

I had a client who owned a piece of property near Miami Beach, Florida. One day he came into my office to tell me that he had a purchaser for the property and he wondered if I would handle the transaction on his behalf. This should have been a very simple matter. All I had to do was contact the purchaser's attorney and assure him that we would send the deed as soon as they wired the funds for the purchase price. Rather than handle this transaction in the normal course of business, I came up with an alternate plan. I suggested that he and I fly down to Miami Beach for a getaway. We could sell the property, play some golf, have dinner, and even fly over to the Bahamas to visit a casino. Ron thought that sounded like a great idea and we set up the trip.

Every phase of the excursion went just as we planned. We sold the property, played a round of golf, had a wonderful dinner, and flew to the Bahamas that evening to spend a few hours at the casino. After returning to Michigan, I told many people everything about the trip, except the excursion to the casino. That was a lie. If a person intentionally withholds information about some conduct he or she does not want other people knowing about, that is *a lie of omission*. The foundation of any addiction is built upon lies. I started building the foundation of my compulsive gambling addiction on that trip.

Later that year, Jane and I decided to take a trip to Las Vegas for a vacation. My father always talked about how much fun it was, and he used to say that it was one of the cheapest places for a vacation "if you didn't gamble." Jane, of course, had not been present at Dr. Smith's lecture on cross-addiction so she did not know the danger that gambling posed for a person who had addiction issues. Unaware of any correlation between alcoholism and gambling, she thought the trip sounded like a good time.

A few weeks before we left, I received a call at my office from a friend who was the president of one of our local banks. He asked if we could meet for lunch and I agreed. At the lunch, he told me that he had heard we were going to Vegas, and asked if I would be interested in learning what a person has to do in order to be rated as a "high roller." My heart immediately began to quicken. I couldn't wait for his advice. He told me the first thing I should do was purchase a book on blackjack and learn how to play basic strategy perfectly. After I mastered that, he said to inform the casino where I was staying that I wanted to be "rated as a blackjack player." To receive the highest rating, one must play for at least three consecutive nights, four hours each night. During this period, the player must bet a minimum of $100 per hand. If a player is able to accomplish this, he or she will receive the rating of "high roller." As a high roller, the individual can expect all expenses for future trips to any casino to be paid in full by the casino.

It is impossible to describe the exhilaration I felt following that lunch. I immediately purchased every book I could find on blackjack and had them stacked by the side of my bed. I could not wait to arrive home from work, have dinner, watch a few obligatory TV shows, and get into bed so I could start studying and refining my blackjack skills. Refinement of these skills led to card counting, which meant practicing with five decks of cards. I studied money management systems and betting systems. Hours and hours were spent preparing for my weekend in Vegas, and I loved every minute of it. I had not anticipated anything as much as this since my early days of drinking.

Our first trip to Vegas was a life-altering event. I understood the joy experienced by a 10-year-old boy who is about to embark upon his first vacation in the Magic Kingdom. It was difficult to get a good night's sleep for the entire week before our journey because of the euphoria I was experiencing. The charter flight was nonstop from Detroit, and every seat on the plane was occupied. There was an electric sense of anticipation that something wonderful was about to happen. We participated in a raffle on the flight. Each passenger was invited to write his or her seat number on a five-dollar bill and deposit it in a bag supplied by the attendant. Just before we landed, a young girl was asked to pick one bill out of the bag, and the person sitting in that seat was awarded all the money. It was a wonderful way for some lucky individual to start the trip.

Getting off the plane and walking into the airport was like arriving at an amusement park. We immediately were greeted by the music and lights of the slot machines. With more than half an hour to wait for our luggage, we purchased $50 in tokens so we could play the slots for the first time. Pulling the lever and watching the spinning of the reels was intoxicating, and the sound made by the tokens falling into the metal tray was addicting. After losing the $50, we retrieved our luggage and found a cab to drive us to our hotel. We left a cold and wintry Michigan to arrive in Las Vegas where there were blue skies and temperatures in the 80s.

When we arrived at our hotel, the desk clerk said it would be another two to three hours before our room was ready. He suggested we leave our luggage with the bellhop and spend the time familiarizing ourselves with the property. We walked by the blackjack pit, the baccarat tables, the roulette wheels, the craps tables, and the slots area. We next entered the VIP room, where I would spend most of my gambling time. Everywhere we looked, lights were flashing, bells were ringing, and people were having fun. Las Vegas was everything I had dreamed it would be.

When our room was ready, we returned to the front desk and requested the key, but the clerk informed us that our luggage already had been delivered. Our room was elegant, on the tenth floor with a beautiful view of the Strip and the mountains in the background. We both were exhausted from the long day, but at the same time looking forward to our first night in Vegas which promised dinner and a show. We unpacked, took a short nap, and dressed for the exciting evening ahead.

The first show we saw in Las Vegas was "Siegfried and Roy," one of the most famous magic acts in the history of Vegas. In their signature finale, they brought an elephant on stage and made it disappear. The people in the audience were absolutely amazed. On the way out of the show, my wife asked how they were able to do that. The only explanation I could suggest was, "It was magic."

My first experience associated with good luck in Las Vegas had nothing to do with gambling. My wife and I were walking from one casino to another when she noticed that one of her diamond earrings was missing. We probably had walked several miles by this time, and the thought of retracing our steps seemed daunting. However, back we went, and there, in the middle of the street, sparkling in the lights, was her earring. The chances of finding it were slim, but we were in the mystical world of Vegas, where anything was possible. Our next unbelievable stroke of good fortune occurred on our second day as we were sightseeing in the Barbary Coast Casino on the Vegas Strip. We decided to stop and play two slot machines that stood side by side. We each took $100 in dollar tokens, and after a few pulls Jane hit a $1,000 jackpot. While the bells were ringing and lights were flashing, I, too, hit a $1,000 jackpot. We both screamed and hugged each other as we waited for our payoffs. Any doubts I might ever have had about having "good luck" were erased. From that moment on, I knew I had been touched by the hand of God.

After three days of playing blackjack, the casino host informed me that I had been rated as a *high roller,* which meant that all future gambling excursions would be paid for by the casino that invited us. I no longer remember if I won or lost money on that particular trip; more likely that means I broke even. The entire experience was far more exhilarating than I ever imagined it could be, and the rush I experienced when I was gambling was only equaled by the rush I used to experience from drinking.

A few months after the Vegas trip, Jane and I received an invitation to visit Harrah's Resort and Casino in Lake Tahoe, Nevada. We were informed that all expenses of the trip would be paid ("comped") by the casino because I was a high roller.

There were no direct commercial flights into Lake Tahoe, so the first leg of our trip was a flight to Reno. As we walked into the airport in Reno, we noticed a man holding a sign over his head that read "Mr. and Mrs. Burke." This was our limousine driver. The limo was a stretch, loaded with everything that one could imagine, and it was there for us alone. The 45-minute ride from Reno to Lake Tahoe is through a desolate desert, then up the side of a mountain, with little more than rocks and dead vegetation visible. However, when we got to the top of the crater and looked down, we saw one of the most beautiful sights I have ever seen in my life. Tahoe sits in a lush valley surrounded by snow-capped mountains.

Upon our arrival at Harrah's, we were directed to the VIP desk. The bellhop took our bags and escorted us to our suite, which was beautiful. There was a large gift basket on the dining room table filled with fruits, candy, and cheeses. In the bedroom was a TV set that came out of the floor with a simple flip of the switch. All I could relate this to was the scene in the movie *Annie,* where Little Orphan Annie finally leaves the orphanage to live at Daddy Warbucks' house. As she is standing inside the beautiful mansion looking all around, she declares, "I think I'm going to like it here." That is exactly how I felt; I knew I was meant for the life of a high roller.

It was on this particular trip that I began that deceitful practice that continued for all future gambling excursions. Before I can go into my deceit, I must digress and explain a few things about Jane. Over the years, I have represented hundreds of alcoholics. For some unknown reason, many of these people have spouses who do not have any addictive tendencies. Jane is one of those people; she does not have an addictive bone in her body. I specifically remember times going out to dinner when we were dating or first married. I would always have three or four drinks with my dinner and if Jane ordered a drink, she would never have more than one. I could never figure out why she did that. No one could get a buzz from just one drink. Why would a person even bother having one drink? I saw it as a total waste of alcohol.

Some nights she would order a drink and end up drinking only half of it. That would make me crazy. As we were leaving the table, I always wanted to reach over and grab her drink and finish it for her. I was convinced that the busboy would probably drink it after we left. I have not had a drink in almost thirty years, but the thought of a single drink still perplexes me.

Jane felt the same way about gambling as she did about drinking. She enjoyed making the trips out west; she enjoyed the hotels, spas, food, and shows, but she didn't care for the casinos. In the early days of our trips, I attempted to get her interested in playing the dollar slot machines. If I had been winning, she might play a little. She simply could not stand losing the money. She also said she did not like playing the slots because the dollar tokens would make her hands turn black. I knew before the trip to Tahoe that if these trips with Jane were to continue, I could not lose any money gambling.

When we went to Tahoe, I brought an extra $4,000 that I did not tell Jane about. On the trip home, when the captain asked if there were any winners on the plane, I raised my hand, everyone applauded, and I gave Jane the $4,000. She was delighted! The casino picked up all our expenses, we had experienced a wonderful time, and we even "made" a bunch of money gambling. It was good being the spouse of a high roller.

Over the next fifteen years, we normally would take one vacation a year to a gambling destination. It was a rare trip that I would win money, but of course no one knew that because I always said I had won. The biggest lie that gamblers tell is that they won money. The second biggest lie is when they tell people they broke even. Gamblers lose. Gamblers must lose. The more they gamble, the more they lose.

Every game in the casino is subject to the certainty known as the *house edge*. The casino has a mathematical advantage in all table games, an advantage known as *odds*. The odds, a statistical certainty, *always favor the house*. Any person can beat the odds in the short term, but if a person plays that game over a sustained period of time, *the house must win*. It is this critical truism that escapes the compulsive gambler. If there ever came a time when the casino discovered the house edge was no longer in their favor, that game would be stopped immediately. It's that simple.

The mechanical games such as slots are controlled by a computer chip. The casino determines what amount of money will be paid out by each machine and what amount will be retained by the casino. Today, 70 percent of the casino's profits come from the slot machines. These machines are developed by people who are experts in the field of psychology. They understand what they have to create to appeal to the gambler, to keep him or her playing.

Most compulsive gamblers have two traits in common. First, they believe they are smarter than anyone else, and possess a knowledge and understanding of the game that is far superior to the other gamblers. Second, they believe they have been blessed with the glorious gift they choose to call "luck," which guarantees riches beyond their wildest imaginations. For the gambler who spends considerable amounts of time at the casino, these traits are reinforced continually by events of the day. Problem gamblers all have a "system" for beating the house. In the rare instances when the gambler does win, that event serves to reinforce his or her belief that their system works.

I personally have witnessed unexplainable runs of luck. These are the episodes the gambler chooses to remember and to tell everyone. Gamblers avoid discussing times when they have lost everything; gamblers suffer from an affliction known as *selective memory*. If gamblers are honest with their friends and loved ones, and tell them that they had been losing money day after day at the casino, those friends and loved ones are likely to suggest that the gambler stop going to the casino. No matter how deep the hole, the gambler always believes there is the possibility of a win big enough to cure the problems created by the gambling. It was this dream that allowed me to return to the casino day after day, regardless of the fact that I lost the majority of the times I gambled.

One year, Jane and I were invited to a New Year's celebration at the Hilton in Las Vegas. The idea of spending New Year's Eve in Vegas was very exciting and we jumped at the invitation. The Hilton actually was located quite far off the Strip, making it very difficult to walk to any other casino from there. It is a huge facility, probably best known as the venue where Elvis performed. On New Year's Eve, high rollers fly in from around the world and converge for a night of gambling and partying, a great night to be in Las Vegas.

On New Year's Eve, the blackjack tables were divided into groupings and each had a minimum bet amount, ranging from $100 all the way to no limit. The smallest bet that could be placed in the casino that night was $100. The women dressed in beautiful evening gowns and furs and the men dressed in tuxedos. Every table in the casino was packed with players, and every person was there by invitation only. As guests checked in, they were given a Sony Watchman television as a gift from the hotel. My most vivid memory is that I couldn't do anything right at the blackjack tables. I kept losing hand after hand. I did not have one single run of good luck the entire time we were there. I felt as though I was trapped in the Hilton for the entire weekend and could not escape to any other casino. I took a major beating. After we returned home, my wife prominently displayed the little Sony TV we had been given. For years, I had to endure looking at that thing every time I walked into the den—of course, I was the only one who knew that our "free" gift actually cost $10,000.

We also were invited to vacation at a casino on Paradise Island in the Bahamas. The island was spectacular, the ocean beautiful, and the weather sunny and warm. Everything was perfect except my luck at the blackjack tables. By the second day of our trip, I was tapped out, so I called our bank back home to ask them to wire me money. As it turned out, I eventually lost most of the money that had been wired that day.

As we were leaving to go home, the casino accounting department notified me that I had not played the requisite number of hours a day to receive a comp and therefore I would be expected to pay all the expenses we incurred while in the Bahamas. They explained their comps were based solely on time played, and not on money lost. I was livid.

There was a very interesting law in effect on the island at that time: No resident was allowed to gamble in the casino. I was told they did this to protect their own people. *What do they know in the Bahamas that we don't know here?*

Over the years, my wife and I enjoyed several genuinely pleasant times in Vegas and the Bahamas—excellent meals and great shows. We took fun drives through the desert to visit Laughlin and the Hoover Dam, and we even took a helicopter ride to the bottom of the Grand Canyon, where we enjoyed a picnic lunch. On a couple of occasions, we took our daughters with us.

Unfortunately, each trip was tainted by my constant lying about how much I gambled. The foundation of my compulsive gambling addiction grew stronger with each trip west.

If the trips with my wife caused financial difficulty, I would have to say the trips with my brothers caused financial devastation. When the three of us traveled to Vegas, I was out of control.

The adrenaline rush was so great that for five days and four nights, I required little or no sleep. Our room, food, and golf rounds were all comped because I was a high roller. My brothers thought everything was free, and they had no idea of the amounts of money I lost in the casino. Neither was a big gambler, so they would go up to the room early for a good night's sleep to be rested for golf the following day while I would stay down in the casino and gamble most of the night.

On a normal day, we would enjoy a decadent breakfast, and then be off for a round of golf at the Desert Inn Golf Course. If the course was busy, I would tip the starter a black chip ($100) and we would be the next group called. After golf, we had lunch followed by a relaxing time in the spa with hot tubs, saunas, and massages on request. After the spa, my brothers would return to the room to rest for a few hours while I played blackjack in the casino. Every evening, we would find some great restaurant and eat like kings. After that, it was back to the Desert Inn for a couple of hours of gambling. My brothers usually would retire for the day around midnight, and I would stay at the casino and gamble for the rest of the night. The next day, we would complete the same routine over again. Unfortunately, the more time I spent gambling, the more money I lost.

On one of these trips, I was in the casino at about 3:00 A.M. when I ran out of money. I found an ATM and took a $2,000 cash advance on one of my credit cards so I could continue gambling. About an hour later, I went upstairs for a little rest, and as I entered the room, our phone was ringing. It was Jane calling from home, and she was worried to death. The credit card company had just called to make sure it was one of us who had taken the cash advance. I had been caught, and I could not lie my way out of it this time.

Fortunately, I always was able to recover financially from my yearly gambling trips. Over the course of the year, I could pay off all my debts and stock up for the next excursion. I honestly believe I could have survived this lifestyle for a few more years had it not been for the changes that took place in 1994 with the opening of Casino Windsor.

The greatest pitfall for any compulsive gambler is proximity. Numerous studies have been conducted that show when a new casino comes into an area, all problems associated with compulsive gambling are doubled for those who live within fifty miles. Howell is fifty-eight miles from Windsor.

Immediately after Casino Windsor opened in 1994, I started making a couple of trips a week to Canada to gamble. Normally, I would take $200 to $300 a trip. It was easy to convince myself that I could afford to spend this at the casino because I was making a good living and did not see my gambling as a problem. Unfortunately, the reality of the situation was much different from my fantasy world. I was losing $600 a week; that works out to over $30,000 a year. Like any other addiction, I had to gamble more to attain the same high. After three or four years, I found myself in an unbelievable situation. As a direct result of my many trips to the casino, I was broke. I had maxed out all my credit cards, had secretly mortgaged our house, and was heavily in debt to my bank. I was even making a point to come home at noon so I could get to the mailbox and remove any suspicious bills or those that could not logically be explained.

My solution was to contact an old client and try to borrow some money. I had represented a couple who had won a state lottery and did not want that information made public. I established a blind partnership that could receive proceeds each year for twenty years. After receiving the monies, the partnership would pay all the taxes, put some of the money in an investment account, and pay the rest over to my clients. This was the perfect solution because no one would ever know they had won the lottery.

I told them I was having financial problems and needed to borrow $75,000. There was not one second of hesitation. They told me they understood and not to worry, and they wrote out the check. The only thing they asked in return was a simple promissory note.

It was the first of many occasions on which I took advantage of my position as friend and counselor to obtain money with which to gamble. I did use some of this money to get the wolves off my back, but a good part of it was lost at the casino. I now was entering the phase of gambling known as *chasing*, meaning that I was attempting to win back the money that I lost at the casino.

A few months after that loan was made, the same clients came to see me because they wanted a divorce. I agreed to handle it for them. When they divided their property, the wife ended up taking the promissory note I had signed. She knew I was having financial troubles, so she always gave me money. She said being able to help me out financially made her feel good. I took the money every time. She had no idea that I was gambling or that I was shamefully taking advantage of her generosity.

This deceit continued for nine months until she finally realized that I was unable to pay her back. She became furious, and I did not think I would ever hear from her again, but that was not the case. A few weeks later, I received a call from an attorney in another city. He informed me that he was now representing my former client, and that they demanded to see me the following day at 4:30 P.M. in his office to discuss the $300,000 I had stolen from her. I had absolutely no idea how much she had given me over the past nine months because my only concern when I got the money was to obtain as much as I could to continue my gambling.

As I walked into his office the following day, she was sitting at the conference table with her attorney. To this day, I remember my righteous indignation as I explained I had never stolen anything; the money had been a gift. The attorney looked at me and smiled. He told me we wouldn't have to worry about that because his client would file a grievance with the state bar and they could make the determination of how I obtained my client's funds. He also informed me he was going to file a suit on behalf of his client to recover the $300,000, and that the local paper would have a field day with such a good story. I became aware right then that I would have to work out some type of arrangement or my life as I knew it would come to an end.

Over the next few months, we arrived at an agreement wherein I would pay my client the sum of $100,000 up front and the balance at the rate of $15,000 twice a year until paid in full. My immediate problem was that I didn't have any money, and there was no way I could borrow $100,000. The only place I could obtain that amount of money was from my clients' trust accounts. A trust account is made up of funds from divorces, personal injury actions, and estates. Every attorney knows that under no circumstances can a client's funds be removed from that account without the client's express permission. To do so is illegal and a violation of the lawyer's oath. Like the majority of compulsive gamblers, I committed a crime to get money because of the problems my gambling had caused.

I wrote the check out of a client's trust account to make the initial payment of $100,000. I told myself that I was simply borrowing the money and that I would return it as soon as I could. I had no intention of depriving my clients of any money! I simply needed to use it for a short time until I could replace it. Of course, there was no place that I could come up with that type of money except back at the casino. Because I had no money of my own with which to gamble, it meant I would have to keep taking more out of the trust account until I *was* able to repay the account with my winnings. During the next two years, I cashed hundreds of checks from that account to finance my gambling. I was constantly robbing Peter to pay Paul. The clients who complained the most were paid their money. I would settle a case and use a part of those funds to pay off some other client I owed, and I would use the rest to gamble in the hopes of winning enough to repay the funds taken out of the trust account.

In July 1998, construction was completed on the permanent casino and Hotel Windsor, and I was invited to attend the grand opening. When I arrived, the casino was operating at full capacity. Something happened that night to change how I felt about blackjack for a long time to come.

All the tables in the casino were crowded, including those in the VIP pit. Wayne Newton was the star attraction that night. They brought him into the pit and made sure all the high rollers were introduced to him. That, of course, included me. I finally found an opening at a $100 minimum/$2,500 maximum table. I was the third spot on the dealer's left; every other chair was taken. I had been playing for a little over an hour and I was doing very well.

Descent 3

Victim Quote:
"I don't understand how Mr. Burke can embezzle money for so long and nobody knew about it. I don't understand it . . . and he's been through alcoholism, everything else, and everybody has problems. . . .

He stopped the alcoholism. Why didn't he stop the gambling?"

Then came "The Hand."

My luck was running well that night. I increased my minimum bet as I continued to win. I now was betting $500 a hand. On my next hand, I was dealt two eights. The dealer showed a six. Basic strategy demands that I split the two eights and play two hands. I split the eights and had to wager another $500. The next card dealt to me was another eight. I put in another $500. The dealer proceeded to turn up another eight. I put in $500 more and was now playing four separate hands. The next card was a three, and I doubled down for $500—my next card was an eight.[1] The next card dealt was another three and I doubled down again for $500. This time I drew a nine for a total of twenty. On the third eight, the dealer gave me a two and I invested another $500 to buy a face card. On the final eight, I got another two, put in $500 more, and once again received another face card from the dealer. I now had one hand that totaled nineteen, three hands that totaled twenty, and wagers that totaled $4,000.

All the other players except a gentleman sitting at third base (closest to the dealer) had passed. He had a twelve showing against the dealer's six. For some reason, he decided to take a hit and the dealer dealt him a ten, and took his one $100 chip. When *the dealer revealed his hole card to be a ten, I simply stared at the guy seated at third base in wonder and amazement. I knew at that moment that I was going to lose the biggest bet I had ever made in my life. Fate was about to trample me and there was nothing I could do. My destiny had been left in control of an idiot who didn't understand basic blackjack. I would have bet $10,000 that the dealer's next card would be a five. IT WAS. The dealer now had twenty-one, and everyone at the table lost.*

I have never questioned another person at a blackjack table as to why they did or did not do something. I could not restrain myself this time. I asked the player why he took a hit on twelve against a dealer who was showing a six. He candidly stated that he thought he could make his hand better.

I left the table and asked a valet for my car. The drive home from the casino that night was the longest I had ever experienced.

A few months after the permanent casino at Windsor opened, I received a call from one of my lawyer buddies, asking if Jane and I would like to go to Casino Windsor on the following Saturday for dinner and a little gambling. I had no concerns about going and being recognized because I normally gambled in the daytime and rarely on a weekend. We agreed to go. That Saturday, my friend drove and pulled into the valet parking at the casino. As we exited the car, one of the valets who usually worked the day shift was parking cars that evening. He looked over at me and said, "Good evening, Mr. Burke. Good luck tonight!" My friend simply looked at me and smiled. It was obvious to him that this was not my first trip to the casino. At the first opportunity, my wife wanted to know how I knew that young man. I explained that I had been there a few weeks earlier after attending a meeting and had given him a generous tip for getting my car. The lies continued.

Because of my addiction to gambling, my law practice was being destroyed. I was spending less time in the office, ignoring my clients' problems, and taking more and more money out of my clients' escrow accounts. I was doing everything in my power to settle cases quickly so I could take funds to pay off those clients who were clamoring for their money. What was left would be taken to the casino. I was always short of money. One morning, while on my way to the casino, I called the office to leave a message for my secretary. A recorded message informed me that there was a problem with my phones that should be fixed shortly. I called the phone company to see what the problem was, and they informed me that the phones had been turned off for failure to pay a $30 bill. They directed me to a nearby store where I could make a payment in cash and have the phones turned back on. As I was standing at the counter paying the bill, I noticed the look on the clerk's face as he tried to figure out how I had gotten myself into such a pitiful situation.

The last two years of my addiction, I made the drive to Windsor an average of three to five days a week. Everything I did was scheduled around gambling. I purposely signed up for cases that would allow me to appear at courts that were in close proximity to the casino.

The gamut of emotions was unbelievable. On the way to the casino, with money in my pocket, I fantasized tremendous winnings and paying back all the money I had taken. Each time I had no doubt that this would be the day it would all turn around, and I would start winning again. Then, on the way home, I screamed at the top of my lungs, cursing the bad luck that was not allowing me to win. Every day of my life, I was forced to lie to everyone important to me to protect my addiction.

One day, I lost about $4,000 playing blackjack, and I was in a terrible state of depression. All I wanted to do was find a spot to have a cup of coffee. I wanted to be away from the tables and take a moment to clear my head. I sat down at a $5 slot machine and ordered my coffee. When the slot attendant came by, I purchased a roll of tokens. I put the first two tokens in the machine, pulled the lever, and all of a sudden lights were flashing and bells were ringing. I had hit the jackpot. For $10, I had just won $12,500!

As I sat there waiting to be paid, God spoke to me. God told me that the answer to all my financial problems was the slot machines. In the next few months, I progressed from the $5 to the $20, and finally to the $100 machines. Winning and losing no longer had anything to do with my trips to the casino. Everything now revolved around being *in action*. The only time I felt safe was when I was sitting at a slot machine and playing.

The first time I won a $100,000 slot was on a $20 machine. The excitement of that win was staggering. My family was out of town for the weekend at a dance convention. I rarely went to the casino after 5:00 P.M. because I did not want them to know I was gambling, but on an occasional weekend like this one, I would sneak over for a good part of the time my family was gone. Jane told me they would call from their hotel room when they arrived in Chicago. I had been at the casino most of the afternoon, but made the one-hour drive home about 7:30 P.M., so I was at the house when they called to tell me about their adventures that day and about the wonderful time they were having. I made up something about what I had been doing and confirmed that our next call would be after the competitions on Saturday night. I stayed at the house until shortly after midnight, and then drove to the casino, knowing that I had almost twenty hours of uninterrupted gambling to enjoy.

That night I was having an exceptional run of luck on the $5 slots, so I took $2,000 of my winnings and tried playing the $20 slot machines. I had been playing for a few hours and was basically staying even, playing two machines. I was playing two triple-diamond machines when the bells started ringing and the lights started flashing. The machine on my left hit a jackpot; I hadn't even noticed! The person next to me did and started yelling and screaming and hugging me. I had won my first $100,000 jackpot.

The next hour was wonderful. The technicians checked out the machine, and I simply stood around waiting to be paid. Everyone wanted to shake my hand and congratulate me. Some people actually walked up and touched me, in hopes that some of my luck might rub off. "What was I going to buy with the money?" they asked. Little did they understand that it had nothing to do with acquiring material goods; it was all about the gambling. I took it in cash—one hundred $1,000 bills. What a rush! About $4,000 went in tips to casino personnel. It was fun acting the role of a big shooter with their money.

I now wanted to test how good my luck was running, so I decided to play some high-stakes blackjack. I bought twenty $1,000 chips. My idea was to play a thousand a hand and increase my winnings. It took about a half hour to lose the entire $20,000. After that, I went back and played more $20 slots.

I left the casino so I could be home by 6:00 P.M. in case there was an early call from my family in Chicago. After that many hours of gambling, I also needed to bathe. I stayed home until they called and then drove back to the casino to gamble some more. When I returned to the casino, I discovered that I was fully committed to the $20 slots and would never again play the $5 slots. The high that I used to feel from the $5 slot machines now was gone. I also continued to play blackjack at $100 a hand.

The last year of my gambling, I was unable to get a full night's sleep. I would lie with my eyes open late into the night, trying to figure some way out of this insanity. Each night would end the same way. My only solution was to go back to the casino and attempt to win enough money to repay what had been taken from my clients' accounts. One definition of insanity is to continue to do the same thing over and over and expect a different result. Every day of my life had become a paradigm of insanity.

My depression was unbearable because I lived in constant fear that my family would discover my other life. During this time period, both my daughters and my wife would ask me on occasion if I was feeling well. During one apparently bad day, my younger daughter actually demanded that I get a physical. However, by the time these inquiries were made, I had established my busy work patterns and excuses. Like most compulsive gamblers, I became an expert at hiding my addiction. The greatest difference between a substance abuse addiction (alcoholism) and a process addiction (gambling) is that there are no outward signs of the process addiction. There is no odor, no loss of coordination, and no slurring of words. Friends and family of the gambler usually do not see the signs of compulsive gambling until after the gambler has lost everything.

In the fall of 2000, I was sitting at my desk one night, holding a cocked .38 caliber gun to my head. It was the single greatest feeling of relief I had ever experienced. I knew at that moment that all the pain I had been enduring was about to come to a merciful end, and I would no longer have to fear the humiliation of being exposed for the person I had become. As I turned my chair away from my desk, I saw a picture of my wife and two children on my credenza. By this point in my life, my thinking was so sick that I honestly thought they could deal with a suicide more easily than dealing with the man I had become. People commit suicide all the time. However, upon further reflection, I wondered what would happen to them a few weeks later when they discovered all the missing money. That would be too much for them to handle.

Nevertheless, I did have another option at that time. Perhaps there was a way I could end my life and no one would know it was suicide. I had been experiencing excruciating chest pains for quite some time and I knew I was having serious heart problems. With this knowledge, I devised a plan that seemed foolproof. Every Monday night, I had to take the "Mr. Rubbish" cart the hundred yards from the garage to the road for the next day's pickup. I added bricks to the cart so it would be harder to push through the snow. The exertion often took me right to my knees. I could feel my heart trying to burst. I was going to commit *suicide by garbage*. The beauty of the plan was that no one would ever know it had been intentional. Now my family would only be forced to confront the issue of the missing money. Unfortunately, this strategy continued to fail week after week.

On three more occasions I won $100,000 jackpots. What each of those wins meant was simply a guarantee of another four days during which I didn't have to worry about where I would find the money to gamble. I could gamble for six or seven hours a day for four days and not worry about anything else. Those were the best of times.

During the last two months of my gambling, I lost $600,000 at the casino. The most significant aspect of that to me is that I have no memory of actually gambling or being inside the casino. I remember everything else. I drove to five or six different banks each day to withdraw the needed funds. The pockets of my suit coat bulged with the thousands of dollars I took each day. The time spent inside the casino was erased by a blackout, just like those I used to experience when I was drinking. Looking back, the number of similarities between drinking and gambling was astonishing.

Finally, on March 30, 2001, it all came to an end. That morning I went to the state bar of Michigan and reported what I had been doing with my clients' funds. After that, I traveled the few additional miles to the state attorney general's office. There, I gave a full statement to one of the criminal attorneys, and he arranged for my arraignment in court the following week. The remainder of that day I drove around, trying to decide how I could tell my family. Jane had no idea that I was living a double life. She knew that finances were tight, but she attributed it to a downturn in my law practice. Her father had been a sole practitioner, so she was well aware of the feast-and-famine aspects associated with this type of practice. She also knew I gambled, but had no idea of the extent. There are no physical signs of compulsive gambling— no odors, no stumbling, no slurred speech. Because she had her own job and finances, household bills were always paid. In most instances, when a gambling addiction finally is discovered, the damage that has already been done is catastrophic. The sense of betrayal is devastating. The person can never be trusted again.

By then, Jane and I had been together for over thirty years, and we were still best friends. We each had careers we loved: mine the

law and hers special education. We always seemed to agree on issues with the girls, and in those few cases in which we didn't, we
were able to provide a unified front; we always supported each
other. We both were involved in the girls' activities. We knew and
enjoyed their friends and cherished the times they spent at the
house. How could I tell Jane about the terrible pain our daughters
were about to suffer?

I arrived at the house before Jane came home from school that
day. As I waited for her, the minutes seemed like hours. She walked
into the living room, and I told her I had something terrible to tell
her. She sank into a chair as the horror of the moment enveloped
her. As I told my story, she simply stared right through me. She was
going into a state of shock right before my eyes. At some point, she
instinctively started contemplating what effect this would have on
our daughters. Immediately, they were her only concern. She knew
everything was about to turn real bad real fast, and she was determined to do everything in her power to protect our children. She
called her sister, who lived a hundred miles away, and asked her to
be at our house when I told our younger daughter. She next had me
call my brothers and sisters and tell them the whole story.

Katey came home that night about seven o'clock, happy with
her fun day of looking for a prom dress. She was a junior in high
school, just sixteen years old. We had a special father-daughter relationship. Some fathers go through difficult times with their
daughters, but we never experienced that. Katey is one of the most
honest, moral people a person could ever meet and demands that
trait in the people close to her. She was one of the most popular
kids in her school and loved by those who knew her. She often let
us know how happy she was with her life and how she hoped
nothing in it would change.

As I told her the story, tears ran down her face, and she kept
repeating that it couldn't be true. When I finished, she turned to
her mother and asked, "Are you going to allow this man to stay in
this house?" Later, her boyfriend picked her up and took her to his
house where she was met by a close group of friends.

A short time later, my brother-in-law drove me to Ann Arbor, where Amy was a senior at the University of Michigan. She and I sat in the back seat as he drove us back to the house, and I told her the story. In an effort to comfort me, she kept rubbing the back of my hand and assuring me that someday everything would be okay again.

We all reacted in our own ways. As I sat in the living room that night, I knew our lives had been changed forever. None of it made any sense. No one in my family deserved any of this. It was difficult to breathe. I knew perfectly well what the next few months held in store for me and my family. I had destroyed the lives of every person who was important to me—and for what reason?

The next few days were an out-of-body experience. Although I was watching what transpired around me, I was numb in my reaction. I was living in a nightmare. I wanted to wake up and have my life back again. The weekend was spent talking to family and friends, trying to explain what occurred and what we thought the future might hold. No one in the family had any idea of the insanity that had been going on. Most had no idea how to respond.

I also contacted several of the victims to tell them personally that I had taken their money out of my trust account and gambled it away at the casino. One of the families I had known all my life. When I was twelve years old, I was their paperboy, and I attended school with their children. I went to their house on Saturday morning and told them everything that had happened. Their only concern was for Jane and the children. It was painful watching them attempt to make some sense out of my betrayal.

NOTE

1. There are certain instances in blackjack when the advantage held by the house (casino) over the player can be greatly reduced. In the long run, the house always has a mathematical advantage. If this advantage could ever be manipulated in a manner that would benefit the player, that game would either be altered or removed from the casino. In the short term, anyone can win. In the long run, only the casino will win.

One rule of blackjack that does favor the player is called the *double down*. If a player has two cards that total eleven or less, he can tell the dealer he wishes to double down. The player must double the size of his original bet and he will then receive only one more card. The player will normally choose to double down when the dealer is showing a bust card (meaning greater probability of going over twenty-one)—two through six. It is one of the few instances in blackjack when the player has the advantage over the house.

Arraignment

4

Victim Quote:
"I think there's fraud, deceit, theft, and then the embezzlement. . . . I have trusted this guy with virtually my life.
He was my guardian."

Tuesday, April 2, 2001, was one of the most bizarre days of my life. The agreement with the attorney general was that I would be transported from Howell by a police officer to my arraignment in a neighboring county. All of the judges in the county in which I resided disqualified themselves from my case because I had appeared before them for many years, and we were friends. My file was assigned to a judge in the city of East Lansing who would preside over the hearing.

It was a policy of the department to handcuff defendants when in custody. The officer, who knew me well, placed my overcoat over the cuffs. The driver was another old friend of mine. We'd been involved in a number of cases and enjoyed a good working relationship over the years. I was embarrassed to put them in this position. They attempted to be kind and made small talk on the thirty-mile trip from Howell to East Lansing.

The purpose of an arraignment is to notify the defendant of the crime that he or she is being charged with and to set an appropriate bond. When we entered the courtroom, several family members and a few friends were present. The judge read the charge of embezzlement of a client's funds in excess of $20,000 and asked how I wished to plead. I stood mute and the judge entered a not guilty plea on my behalf. The matter was set for a pretrial at a later date.

When I returned home, family members were there, awaiting my return from court. The phone had not stopped ringing as my story spread throughout our small community. We sat in the living room, and I watched helplessly as my family tried to get a handle on the events as they unfolded. They were all dazed and bewildered by my revelations. One of the pillars of their family had crumbled before their eyes, and they could not make sense of any of it. Everyone wanted to do something to make the situation better, but the situation was not going to get better for a long time.

At some point during the afternoon, my sister asked Jane if there was anything she could do for her, or if there were any concerns she had that needed to be addressed. Jane told her that one thing she had been asking me to do for months was to get a physical. She recounted the numerous episodes when she knew I was having chest pains, but refused to seek any medical help. My sister said she would call around and see if she could find a doctor who would give me a physical. As she was explaining my symptoms to one doctor, he told her that I should be taken to the emergency room immediately to have an EKG. I was in no position to argue about anything at that time and simply did what I was told.

My sister and brother took me to the emergency room at the local hospital, where the staff immediately started me on a heart monitor. The doctor was not aware of my troubles and asked if I had been under any unusual stress. In the next fifteen minutes, I tried to explain as best as I could the recent events in my life that led to my being hospitalized. He responded that stress was a major factor in heart problems, and that my current situation could account for the pains I was experiencing. As we waited for the test results, the doctor told us of his personal problems and the stress and anxiety he was suffering as a result of some newly acquired stepchildren. It appeared that my emergency room doctor had entered into a second marriage complete with stepchildren from hell. He spent the following hour revealing how much he loved his new wife and how much he disliked her children. He understood I was under tremendous stress because of my present situation; however, he left me with the distinct impression that my stress paled in comparison to the stress he was going through. My greatest concern at that point was that my sister was going to burst out laughing. To this day, she still laughs when she tells others the story of my experience with the doctor in the emergency room on the day I was arraigned.

Later that day, I was transferred by ambulance to St. Joseph Hospital in Ann Arbor. Following two days of tests, the doctor informed me that I had three blocked arteries and that surgery was scheduled for the following morning. He wanted me to understand that the situation was very serious and suggested that I visit with my family prior to the surgery.

That night, a Catholic priest came into my room to administer the sacrament of Last Rites. I told the priest to get the hell out of my room. I did not want to be forgiven; I wanted to die and spend eternity in hell. I felt that was the only appropriate punishment for what I had done to my family, my friends, and my victims.

I survived the heart surgery and spent the next eight days in the hospital recuperating. When I finally was released to go home, I was still in fairly fragile shape. As I sat in the living room, I noticed a pile of letters on the coffee table. The first was from the wife of one of my victims from whom I had taken hundreds of thousands of dollars. She wrote to tell me that her father had been a compulsive gambler and had taken money that didn't belong to him to use for gambling. She went on to say that she not only understood my conduct, but that she and her husband forgave me and would pray for my family and me. I was astounded. There has not been one day since then that I have not thought about the empathy shown by that woman and her husband.

Another letter that caught my attention was from Casino Windsor. I wondered if it was a get well card. Instead, the envelope contained a restraining order. This was a court order restraining me from entering the premises of Casino Windsor, because I was an *undesirable person*. They had released a statement to the press that they did not want compulsive gamblers like Michael

Burke at their casino. They wanted only responsible gamblers who were able to control their gambling and who used the casino solely for recreational purposes. Unfortunately, that is not the case; casinos make more than 50 percent of their profits from the problem/compulsive gambler.

I was arraigned on April 2, 2001, and sentenced on June 18, 2001. Between those two dates, I had triple bypass surgery, pled to the crime as charged, and provided the information required for the pre-sentence report. It took approximately seventy-five days to resolve my entire case. I knew this had to be over and done with as soon as possible for the sake of my family. There was nothing to be gained by putting it off. My two attorneys knew what I wanted and followed my wishes, and the process was concluded in record time. The only issue yet to be resolved was sentencing.

Sentencing

5

Victim Quote:
"This is a man that I trusted."

Finally, the day of my sentencing arrived. Jane helped me pick out a suit to wear, but she could not attend. She had been through too much in the past two months and was unable to cope with any more.

I entered the courtroom and sat at the defendant's table with my two attorneys. The room was filled with the people who would later be offering their victim-impact statements. On the other side were my family and friends. My daughters sat next to each other among their aunts and uncles. Instead of jurors, there were TV cameras. Finally, the judge entered the room and we were ready to proceed.

The first people to speak were my victims. Each spoke about the pain I brought into their lives and the financial devastation they incurred because they selected me to represent them in their legal matters. By the time they finished, I was numb. I always had known how horrific my actions were, but to sit and listen to each victim tell his or her story made it even worse.

Now the time had arrived for the judge to sentence me. I felt tremendous remorse for what I had done to my victims, my family, and my friends, but there was no way I could convey to them that I never dreamed it would end with my standing in a courtroom waiting to be sentenced. How could I explain to these people that I always had intended to replace their money? No sentence could be severe enough to punish me for the pain I caused. I remember looking at the judge and feeling terrible about the spot I had put him in as well. No one would find satisfaction on this day.

I was sentenced to serve three to ten years in the Michigan Department of Corrections and was further ordered to pay restitution to my victims in the sum of $1.6 million.

The following excerpts are taken from the transcripts of my sentencing.

The Prosecutor's Remarks

There's two areas that I'd like to cover. The first is it seems more and more often these days at sentencing that we hear the excuse I'm addicted to alcohol. I'm addicted to drugs. Today we heard I'm addicted to gambling. I don't buy the argument, your Honor, that that's a sickness. But even if we do, it's certainly one that has—can be taken care of. In this case both the pre-sentence report and many of the letters that were written on behalf of Mr. Burke state that he has had a longstanding alcohol problem and that he has it under control because he goes to alcoholics anonymous.

Mr. Burke is a bright man, your Honor. He completed seven years of college education after high school. If he has a gambling problem and it truly is a sickness he well knew that he could take care of that problem by getting treatment for it. And he chose not to.

But more important, your Honor, I think is the fact that we need to look at the purposes of sentencing. Two of those purposes are deterrents and punishment. And in this case, I think we need—we need to take a look at both of those. The recommendation is for Mr. Burke to do 90 days in jail and one year on a tether. This on a case where he stole admittedly in excess of one million dollars. If one million dollars doesn't get you sent to prison, your Honor, I don't know what does. I've prosecuted a number of cases where defendants have stolen in excess of a million dollars and in every one of them they went to prison.

In this case, Mr. Burke stole over a million dollars. And I think both to punish him for that and to deter others from following that path, he needs a sentence well in excess of 90 days in jail and a year on tether.

Now I understand that what I'm asking you to do is exceed the guidelines. But the guidelines can be exceeded when there's good reason to do so. And I would note that in scoring the guidelines, you get the same number of points whether you steal $20,000 or a million dollars. Now that leaves an awful wide range where you get the same number of points which are used to determine what your sentence should be. I think in this case because of the amount that was stolen, the sentence should be a term in prison and I would ask you to impose a sentence of two to ten years in the state penitentiary.

Jim Buttrey is a public defender in Howell. He has been a longtime friend and is an excellent attorney. He is best known for protecting the constitutional rights of his clients. He hoped that the court would fashion a sentence in which I would not only spend time in jail, but also would be required to work and use my earnings to make some repayment to my victims.

Jim Buttrey's Comments

Obviously, your Honor, restitution is required in this case. It's required by law. It's required for Mr. Burke to regain not only the respect of the community but his self-respect. And I know the Court has read a lot of letters doubting whether any significant restitution will ever be paid in this case. But I'm suggesting to the Court in light of Mr. Burke's work history and his intelligence there's every reason to believe that substantial restitution is going to be paid on this file.

The bottom line is Mr. Burke must dedicate the rest of his life to making this right, and he knows it.

The question I frankly feel called upon to answer today, your Honor, is why don't you send Mr. Burke to prison? I know that a lot of victims call for it. It seems appropriate. The answer to that question is because the law militates strongly against it. And when we talk about the law and sentencing, we're talking about the guidelines. And those of us who have been doing this long enough we're on our third set of guidelines. And these are new out of 1999. And they've pretty much changed the sentencing landscape to the extent that maybe it's not accurate to call them guidelines as much as to call them strictures.

The Legislature rewrote the entire sentencing policy of this state recently. As they have rewritten the embezzlement statute recently. This statute now contemplates, encompasses a series of acts and imposes no minimum sentence. The minimum sentence is imposed by the guidelines.

And in this case, the guidelines I'd suggest do take into account the major aggravating factors in this case which are points scored for the amount of money. Points are scored for the amount of money. Points are scored for the violation of trust. Points are scored for the continuing course of conduct. And departures from the guidelines— and I've read the pre-sentence report and certainly I anticipate Mr. Walter asking the Court to depart from the guidelines. Unlike under our old law departures are discouraged to say the least. And departures for reasons taken into account by the guidelines are actively discouraged.

When we read the whole set of laws that the Legislature wrote to reduce sentencing, I'd suggest to the Court that the point of these guidelines is to distinguish between the people we're mad at and the people we fear. And Mr. Burke clearly doesn't fall into the latter category. It is apparent how important the Legislature believes these guidelines to be when they write into the law that if a minimum sentence is within the appropriate guidelines range the Court of Appeals shall affirm that sentence and may not overturn it unless the Court's sentence is on inaccurate information or unless the guidelines are wrong. That's how important the Legislature I'd suggest feels these are.

And I'm not suggesting that we're somehow pawns of the Legislature in this room but we are tools of the Legislature. And we've got to do our job. And I'm going to suggest to the Court there are other mitigating factors that are not taken into account by the guidelines.

And one is the motivation behind the crime. And I want to make clear that I offer up no excuse. Mr. Burke's actions were in fact inexcusable. And I recognize and we can't forget, we shouldn't forget, we must not forget that the victims are out their money. It makes no difference to them why it's gone. But I suggest it bears on sentencing.

It is frankly less venial that this money was, went to feed an addiction than if it were stolen to finance a sumptuous retirement or buy a Swiss chalet or scuttled into offshore accounts as Scale Trimble wrote his gambling addiction was so severe that he did these things. Well you can take it further than that. You heard what he loves the most, his family and he threw away everything he worked his adult life for. And that's a legal profession.

And I'm sure the Court's read a letter opining that gambling addiction is three times worse than heroin. I'm not going to pass any comment on that. But I will suggest that in a very important way compulsive gambling is worse than any other addiction device because of the way it permeates society, because of the way the state spends so much taxpayer money it's actively encouraging the citizenry to get a bet down. And we've got the future of the urban renewal of our greatest city banked in no small degree on gambling. And we rest the economic vitality of our Native Americans on gambling.

I can't put it any better than the line in the local paper. It was under Jane Burke's name, my client's wife. "Pathological gambling is a problem which causes great devastation to many families including my own."

None of this lets Mr. Burke off the hook. This is his crime. This is his sentence. He's got it coming. But no other vice is supported now or ever by such state action and I'd suggest as a result there is some mitigation in the societal context in which this occurred.

I'd suggest the guidelines also don't take into account the kind of person Mr. Burke had been for decades. This is not merely a man with no criminal priors. This is a man who was out actively doing good in the community. And the Court's got a sense from it from some of those letters.

I'd touch on a couple of points. One, a better friend to Howell schools you'd be hard pressed to meet. It's well known Mike volunteered his time working to pass bond issues and millages.

From my own experience, and I've been doing only criminal defense work for the last fifteen, sixteen years. And as the Court can appreciate, the majority of my practice deals with the consequences of life spun out of control because of addictions. And what Mr. Burke was good at among the criminal defense bar what he was real good at was getting people into treatment. He knew the places. He knew where he could get clients in, not his clients, other people's clients as well. He sat on the board of Brighton Hospital. To quote my associate Mr. Livingston, hasn't had a drink in more than twelve years, told me out of the blue one day, Mike took me to my first meeting. We'll let the irony of this be lost on no one.

The enormity of this crime, your Honor, has caused ripple effects throughout this small community. We'd like

the Court to know that the good Mike has done throughout the decades he's lived here has also caused a ripple
effect throughout the community. And I'd suggest that
explains the community support that he still has that the
Court sees in those letters. The family support that he has.
The family members are here today. And these are intelligent people. They are not blind to the magnitude of the
crime he's involved in. They hate the sin, and they love
the sinner.

My point is the good that he's done in his life is not
erased by the horrible wrong he's committed. And we're
asking the Court to take it all into account.

And we're asking the Court to take into account as
well his health. As the Court knows, Mr. Burke's a little
more than two months recovered from serious heart surgery, and yet, there were postoperative complications.
And we're asking the Court to take this into account at
sentencing but not as to the severity of any sentence the
Court may impose. And again, I'm asking the Court not
to sentence Mr. Burke to any, out of any sense of pity or
sympathy at all. Our sympathy must lie with the victims.
But the Court I'd suggest must or should be concerned
with the same things Dr. Mallinoff is concerned with. The
ordinary recovering period for an operation of this severity is 60 to 90 days more removed than we are now which
is why I'm suggesting to the Court that regardless of any
sentence the Court imposes allow Mr. Burke to enter and
complete the program we've supplied the Court information on. And even if the Court imposes the maximum
prison sentence today, to allow him to complete that not
only for his mental health but for his physical health as
well.

But again, we're asking the Court not to sentence out
of any sense of pity. We're not asking the Court to ignore
its sense of mercy when there are reasons to support it.

What I'm asking for a sentence in this case is along the lines of what the Probation Department has recommended. But to allow him to enter and complete an inpatient program first. Between inpatient time, jail time, tether time, this Court can impose significant separation from society and significant deprivation of liberty while at the same time maximizing the opportunity for the highest amount of restitution to be paid.

If the Court imposes such a sentence, I'd suggest we can be secure in the knowledge that we followed the law whether we agreed with it or not. And as I'd suggest in this case so important we're dealing with a man who dishonored the law. And every time there's a criminal sentence and the defendant has dishonored the law but this case it runs awful deep. It cuts off awful deep. And I'd suggest our response to it must be to honor the law here today, and we honor the law I'd suggest by scrupulous adherence to it.

I know Mr. Burke was a lawyer, and there's a natural inclination to sentence him more harshly because he was a lawyer. And that inclination I'd suggest is felt to a lesser or a greater degree by every lawyer in this room. I'm asking the Court to resist it. The sentencing law in our state forbids exceeding the guidelines because of an individual's legal occupation. I believe the Legislature meant lawful occupation. But the point's the same. And yet the inclination is natural. In some cases it's strong.

I ask the Court not to sentence Mr. Burke harshly because he was one of us, a lawyer, but to sentence him fairly as you can because he's one of us, a human being.

The Judge's Comments

I would just like to say on the outset here that usually when I pass sentences I don't make a lot of comment. I simply go over the report, let the People make their statements on what they have to say. I then pass a sentence that I feel is appropriate. Occasionally I will make a few comments. I was talking in the back about I've had a particularly bad stretch of cases over the last few months. I just had a gentleman today, for example, who threw a frying pan full of bacon grease all over a lady while she was asleep. Hot bacon grease, of course, that was on the stove. I had a case just the other day where a 12-month-old child was murdered by a boyfriend.

It seems to me that those cases while they are shocking in their own way and those people are going to go to jail, that this particular case to me at least has a certain amount of shock effect. I can honestly sit here and understand why some of these people who stood up today spoke the way they did. Mr. Sadowski is out thousands and thousands and thousands of dollars. Other people are out smaller amounts but in the same respect to them, it's as valuable as what Mr. Sadowski lost.

It seems to me that when I review the guidelines and make a decision on a case that I have to—well, I guess I should say I made a note to myself here. You know, I'm not from Livingston County. I'm from Lansing. Big city over there, and I handle a lot of cases. Actually my office is in Mason, out there in a smaller community. And we try to—when we're judges we try to as best we can reflect the attitudes of the community that we serve with an eye to the fact or with a thought that the state through the Legislature and through the Supreme Court determine a general range of penalties that we should impose on people for conduct. We have to put that range of conduct into context of the situation that we have. And I found it very striking that at least three of the people who spoke to me, Mr. Skinner and a couple of the others commented, very candid . . . . In any event, they commented just as I think frankly as I think to myself when I look at this file I have people who go into a bank and steal $50.00 perhaps with their hand in their pocket pointed at a teller that I send to prison routinely for that conduct because we don't want crimes against people.

And as a general rule, our Legislature has decided that people who commit crimes against property are people who are better off on probation, jail terms, and lesser penalties. There have been people who have gone into banks that I have not sent to prison because of some unusual circumstances. But on the other hand, Mr. Burke, there are people who have committed property crimes that because of their past record and because of any number of circumstances, I have chosen to avoid the guidelines or pass them by with an eye to what they contain and impose a more stringent sentence.

I can honestly say that if the top figure here is anywhere near correct in this case, this is by far the largest embezzlement I've ever had. I've had people taking lots of money. But I've never had anyone steal this kind of money from other people.

And Mr. Buttrey, you commented that you can't sentence someone because of their occupation. I agree with that. I don't sentence anybody because of what they do. I would hope if I was ever in a bad position they wouldn't sentence me for that. But I think that you do have to look at the position of trust that a person is in. I don't choose to put people in positions of trust. They seem to do that for themselves. And when you violate a position of trust, for example, an attorney I had recently was passing drugs with clients in the hallway outside the courtroom. And I was called upon to take that case because judges in another county didn't want to do it. I didn't want to take that case either. But on the other hand, it did strike me as rather unusual to have a client come in here pleading guilty to a felony of delivery of cocaine while you're holding it for them out in the hallway. So that type of a trust position is a difficult one.

Now in this case, I have a situation not the same as that but of a similar type nature where people who are basically—some of these people are obviously disabled individuals or people who need the care of a guardian or someone to overlook their affairs or watch after them. And it appears that Mr. Burke has in fact taken advantage of that situation in a number of different ways. And I think those are factors that I looked at when I reviewed this file.

And when I looked at it I also think that we don't just have a bank in this case although the bank appears to be out a substantial amount of money if they're in a situation I think they're in. Although they're saying one thing today and who knows that they'll say tomorrow. But we have a lot of money, we have a lot of people, and a lot . . . and a corporation or two out a lot of money, a violation of trust, a continuing pattern of conduct for a number of years that was clearly something that at least in my view gambling addiction, okay fine, you can still not drive your car over there.

And I think a very important factor in this case is the fact that I don't believe that in my view there's any likelihood of Mr. Burke ever making any substantial payment towards restitution in this case. I've had people who committed substantial embezzlements who came into court and demonstrated good faith by a large payment towards restitution on the day of sentencing with an agreement with the prosecutor and such but I don't really believe that Mr. Burke will ever have the resources to ever repay this kind of money at least that I can see from this report that indicates he has no assets of any substantial nature whatsoever. So that kind of loss troubles me greatly as well.

So for those various reasons I do believe that the guidelines in this case are not appropriate, and I will accordingly order that Mr. Burke serve a term of 36 months to 120 months with the Michigan Department of Corrections. And a $60.00 Victims Fund Fee.

I failed to hear the arguments of either the prosecutor or my attorney. Everything whirled in my head. The only thing I remember about the judge's sentence was at the time he announced thirty-six months, all the cameras in the jury box immediately panned to my two daughters so no one would miss the emotional devastation through which they were going.

I knew before I left the room that I had to say something to my victims. As an attorney, I learned many years ago that there is nothing anyone can say to convey to a victim how that person feels. My philosophy always has been that it is insulting to apologize to a victim, but it is even more insulting not to apologize.

Michael Burke's Comment

All the victims who are here today, I sincerely apologize for having violated your trust. I know the financial difficulty that I've put you in. And I'm so sorry for having done that. Everyone I've hurt, the victims, and everyone else, I am truly remorseful.

Prison Stories

6

Victim Quote:
"I have worked hard all my life, always obeyed
the law and been good to my fellow man. It just isn't
fair to cheat all of us out of what is rightfully ours.
My wife and I had put our trust in Mr. Burke, and
I am very disappointed in his actions."

One of the oldest, most worn-out jokes that lawyers like to tell each other is, "The client goes to jail; the lawyer goes to lunch." It's how as attorneys we deal with the countless times when our criminal clients received some sort of incarceration for their sentence. It was always the same little "farewell dance": a handshake, maybe some fleeting eye contact, and then we each go our separate ways—the client out the back door, the lawyer out the front door. However, it was a different type of dance for me today.

Immediately after sentencing, I was removed from the courtroom by two deputies and taken to a holding cell. I had to remove my belt and shoelaces and give them to the deputy. This was to assure that there would not be any attempt at suicide. I then was told to hand over all of my personal property. I gave them my wallet, my watch, and my wedding ring. It was the first time I had removed my wedding ring since the day we were married, August 2, 1968. All of these items were put in a bag and given to my attorney, who delivered them to my wife later that afternoon.

Next, I was taken to the county jail to await transport to Jackson Prison. This was the same jail in which I had visited so many of my clients over the years. Now I was the person on the wrong side of the bars, being told to change my civilian clothes for an orange jumpsuit. Most of the county jail cells were filled with young people who had been involved in minor scrapes with the law. The thought of being placed in a cell with these kids was one of the most humiliating experiences of my life, because I deplored the thought of having to explain to them how I had ended up in jail. Thankfully, I was placed in a single medical cell because of my heart condition. I was in the county jail for two days. My meals were brought to me, and I had no contact with any of the other prisoners. Several of the guards who had known me over the years stopped by to check on me, but I was too emotionally unstable to speak with them. I pretended to be asleep when anyone came to see me.

The time arrived for me to be transported, and I made the trip sitting handcuffed in the back seat of a sheriff's patrol car. It was about a one-hour ride on a beautiful summer day. We took the back roads through a number of small communities. My mind wandered as I stared out the window. Each rut we hit jarred me back to the reality of where we were heading. The deputy spoke not one word to me during the entire trip. The only sound came from the crackling of the police radio and the dispatcher's remarks transmitted over the police scanner.

• • •

The journey through the prison system starts at the same place for all inmates; at the Reception, Guidance, and Counseling (RGC) Center. Upon my arrival at the prison, the correctional officers not only took all my medications, they also took my list of medications. Pursuant to prison policy, no medications could come into the prison with an inmate. Instead, all medications had to be ordered by prison physicians to prevent the possibility of unauthorized drugs being brought into the facility.

Inmates first are taken to the shower room, where they are ordered to strip and go through the showers. Then each inmate is subjected to a full-body cavity search and issued a prison uniform. No one talked, and we all simply did as we were told. Before being introduced into the general population, each inmate is given a prison number, and a photo ID is taken. Our final journey from receiving was down a winding corridor to the cell block.

When my group arrived, we were ordered to sit at tables in the middle of the block. There, the correctional officers told us that we would be given the remainder of our clothes and bedding and assigned to our cells. There were tiered cells on each side of the tables at which we were sitting. As I sat there, a feeling of total despair came over me. I closed my eyes and prayed that when I opened them again this would be part of a terrible dream. It wasn't. As we sat there, some of the prisoners who were in the cells yelled obscenities down at us. I was absolutely terrified. I would remain terrified for the next three years.

RGC is the cell block where inmates coming into the system are evaluated to determine where they will be placed within the prison system. Part of that evaluation process consists of reviewing the inmate's past criminal activity and his known assaultive behavior. After the information has been documented, the inmate's final placement is assigned, and he is sent off to serve his time in the appropriate facility.

The entire evaluation process takes approximately thirty days. That period of time is referred to as *quarantine* because the inmate spends the majority of each day locked in his cell. Except for meals and a daily shower, the inmate is allowed out of his cell for only one hour of yard time a day.

During my first week in quarantine, one of the correctional officers stopped by my cell to give me some advice that would remain with me for the entire time I was incarcerated. He told me that if I was going to survive in this environment, I would have to keep my head down and my mouth shut. I listened and followed that advice for the next three years.

• • •

One of the first decisions I had to make was whether to start smoking again. It had been over eighteen years since I had quit. I knew if I started again, my family would perceive this as another betrayal. A few weeks before sentencing, my daughter asked me what I could do to make everything "right" again. I told her I was not sure what the future would hold, but whatever it was, I promised to do the best job I could with the rest of my life. If I started smoking again, my daughter would see it as another broken promise. Smoking was no longer an issue.

• • •

Perhaps the most degrading experience in quarantine was the daily shower. Showers were taken one floor at a time. All the cell doors were opened on the floor, and the inmates would step out wearing a towel. The only items taken to the shower were flip-flop footwear, a bar of soap, and shampoo. The shower room has a long wall with about ten shower heads. Inmates are ordered to stand two deep behind the shower heads. While one prisoner rinsed himself down, the other would lather up. The inmates would then switch, and one would rinse off while the other lathered up. This entire time, the showers were completely surrounded by correctional officers, yelling at the inmates to hurry up and finish. As one group would finish, the next group would take their turn. Some of the officers were women who would stand and watch as the men showered. They were referred to by the inmates as *bone hawkers*. Any remnants of dignity or self-esteem the individual had retained after entering prison were washed away in those showers.

• • •

The evaluation process also included a medical review. At my first appointment, the doctor became furious when he learned that I did not have a list of my heart medications. I tried to explain that not only had the correctional officer taken away my medication, he also had taken the list of medications that I had carried into the facility with me. The doctor told me that I was an idiot for not keeping the list. I tried to explain that it was not a choice that I made, but one that was made for me by prison staff upon my arrival at Jackson Prison. The doctor complained that he would now be put to the great inconvenience of having to contact my heart surgeon to determine what medications had been prescribed so that he could order new medications for me.

• • •

After a few weeks in quarantine, I was called out of my cell for a meeting regarding boot camp. This was the beginning of a saga that lasted almost my entire period of incarceration at Jackson Prison. The boot camp program was established to allow certain prisoners to participate in a military-style program for a ninety-day period in lieu of serving the sentence established by the court. There are prerequisites for eligibility for the program, including that the current felony was the only one the inmate had ever committed, and the maximum amount of time to which the inmate had been sentenced was fewer than three years. Eligibility also depended on the type of felony that had been committed.

A young drill instructor who worked at the boot camp came to the prison and spoke to those who were eligible for the program. She explained what would be required if a person chose to participate in the ninety-day program, and the benefits available if he was able to complete the program.

I asked the drill instructor if they would take someone who recently had undergone heart bypass surgery. She assured me they had to take me because they could not discriminate against any inmate because of a medical condition. I told her I would appreciate an opportunity to participate in the program. She gave me the forms to be filled out so I could be admitted.

The first question was whether the inmate was currently taking any prescription medication. When I told the drill instructor I would be taking medication for my heart, she informed me that I had to be off everything for a period of six months before I was eligible to participate in boot camp. In the beginning of this ordeal, I looked upon this requirement as a positive condition because I now had six months to improve physically. I knew that if I could get in good enough shape to be accepted in boot camp, I would be coming home two years ahead of time. I now had a realistic goal.

•   •   •

The day finally arrived when I was told that I would be transported to my permanent facility. On that day, all my phone privileges were cancelled and none of my mail would be forwarded until I arrived at the new facility. Security for prison personnel required there be no communication with the outside world by an inmate being transported from one facility to another until after he arrived. On the day of the transfer, I was ordered to pack my property and I was taken from my cell to a holding room to await transport. There were forty to fifty other inmates also waiting to be transported to different prisons around the state.

It was a very hot July day and the room had no ventilation. The stench grew worse as the day wore on. I sat there for seven hours, and it was almost unbearable. Finally, they shackled four of us into a van to be transported. As it turned out, the ride to the new facility took less than five minutes. This is where I spent the following three years—Parnell Correctional Facility, a level-one facility that is a part of Jackson Prison. The level of each facility within the prison system is determined by the makeup of the inmate population. To be eligible for a level-one facility, an inmate must be within three years of his early-out date, and he also must qualify as a low-assaultive risk. If a person is at a level one and is involved in aggressive or assaultive behavior, he is returned to a higher level facility and must earn his way back to a level one. There are 1,300 inmates at Parnell housed in four cell blocks.

•   •   •

My new cell block was similar to the one I had just left. I was relieved to learn that all cells were single-man cells. A single cell offered a small degree of privacy and a great deal of security. When that metal door slammed shut, I knew I could not be harmed by other inmates. Both the front and the back of each cell were barred. Inmates could not hang anything on the bars because the correctional officers required an unobstructed view into the inmates' cells at all times. If an inmate was walking down the galley in front of the cells, he never looked into another inmate's "house." This conduct was deemed to be disrespectful, and the consequence for that was physical altercation.

My cell was six feet by eight feet and had a concrete floor. In the rear of the cell were a toilet and a sink. My bed was made entirely of metal and had a hard plastic mattress that was two inches thick. Sleeping in that bed was like sleeping on the concrete floor. The other two articles in the room were a small desk and a locker for clothes. There were strict regulations mandating what personal items were allowed and where those items could be kept in the cell. Inmates were subject to receiving tickets for failure to strictly follow these regulations. With hundreds of inmates in each cell block, garbage was a significant problem. On some nights after the lights were out, I would see shadows of rats running behind the cells. The cell block had been constructed in 1934 and had gone through very few changes since that time. In the winter, it was so cold I would sleep fully dressed, even wearing my coat. In the summer, it was so hot it was like sleeping in a large kiln.

The first thing I did after I arrived at Parnell was to ask the correctional officer at the main desk if it was all right to take a shower. Spending most of the day in a sweltering room left me feeling dirty and sweaty. She informed me that inmates could take showers whenever they wanted. The showers were old, but the spray from the showerhead was powerful and relaxing. I was standing allowing the water to beat down my back, when I turned my head slightly to the left and noticed a person taking a shower three or four showerheads away.

What immediately caught my eye was that this person had breasts. All I could imagine was that somehow I managed to end up in the women's showers and was going to be in a great deal of trouble. Fortunately, as it turned out, the person was a transsexual who went by the name Lindsay. Over time, I found her to be a very decent person.

One personal luxury that an inmate is allowed inside the prison is a television set, which must be purchased from the prison store. There is only one model. It is a nine-inch black and white, made of clear plastic. The purpose of the clear plastic is to make it easy for the correctional officers to look inside and ensure that no contraband is hidden. Inmates also must purchase ear buds to use with the TV. If an inmate is caught using his TV without ear buds, he can be issued a disciplinary ticket. There were eight channels from which to choose. Each set comes to an inmate with his prison number etched into it. If an inmate is found to have a TV without a number, or with a number other than his own, he is given a contraband ticket.

I had been in prison for six months without a television when my sister decided to get one for me for Christmas. She transferred the money into my account so I could buy it from the prison store. When I attempted to make the purchase, I was informed that half the money my sister put into my account had been removed and applied to restitution. She had to put in an identical amount of money before I could make the purchase.

• • •

I was able to arrange a medical appointment shortly after arriving at Parnell and told the doctor of my desire to attend boot camp and the restriction pertaining to medication. She agreed to take me off all medication. It was at that time that I decided to become a vegetarian because I would no longer be taking cholesterol medication. I also started a workout program by walking laps and eventually jogging. After approximately six to nine months of this activity, I felt I was prepared to give boot camp a try and I sent a letter asking to be admitted. I received a response informing me that I would have to be approved by the medical staff at my current facility before I could be accepted.

At that time, I met with the physician's assistant, and we discussed the reality of my attending boot camp. He said that he would put me on a rigorous physical workout schedule, and if I could accomplish the goals he established, he would approve me. One of the goals was that I had to be able to run at least two miles. It would take a year before I was able to accomplish that goal.

• • •

One of the few times a person can "escape" while in prison—figuratively, not literally—is when he receives mail, normally delivered to the cell around four in the afternoon. I would return from my work assignment, hoping to find a letter from family or friends so that for a few moments I could pretend I was with them. However, not all letters were comforting. One day, I found a letter from the State Bar of Michigan on my bed. I knew what it said before I opened it: the final notice of my disbarment. On that day when I first wrote a check out of my client's account, I knew this would be the end result. As I sat on my bed looking at the envelope, my twenty-five years as an attorney flashed before my eyes. Upon reading the contents, I discovered that there was the possibility of reinstatement after payment of the $1.6 million to my clients. I didn't sleep that night. I lay in bed remembering the cases, the clients, my attorney friends, and my life as a lawyer. It all seemed so long ago.

· · ·

My first paying job in prison was as a porter. It was my responsibility to keep the cell block clean. It was a great job because it left me plenty of time each day to work on my physical conditioning. I remember calling my daughter and telling her I had been given a job. She asked me how much it paid, and I told her 86 cents. She said that wasn't a bad hourly rate in prison. I had to inform her that it was 86 cents *a day* and that half of that was paid into a fund for restitution for my victims.

· · ·

One morning, rumors were flying around the yard that there was going to be a general "shakedown" of all cells in the block. That meant that prison personnel would enter each cell and tear it apart looking for contraband. Inmates are always coming up with new ways to manufacture and hide weapons and drugs, so it is up to the prison staff to go through the cells with a fine-tooth comb. This is a never-ending exercise between the inmates and the prison administration. The rumors suggested that the primary purpose was to check on clothing to assure that it was appropriately numbered. A recent decision had been made to put the prisoner's number on each piece of clothing, including shirts, pants, coat, socks, hats, and underwear.

On the night before the alleged shakedown, all porters were told to stay at their stations as the announcement was made that there would be a shakedown the following morning. Any prisoner with more than the allotted amount of clothing would receive a contraband ticket for each piece of extra clothing.

As soon as the announcement was made, clothing came flying down from all four tiers. It looked like blue snow. The porters spent a half hour picking it up and putting it in the dumpsters. The next morning, the announcement was made that the shakedown would begin soon and that this was the last chance inmates would be given to dispose of any contraband. Twenty-five prison officials had arrived to conduct the shakedown. Clothes once again were flying, and the situation was very comical, but I was about to have my first confrontation with the warden.

One prisoner called me to his cell to throw out some stainless steel cleaner that he used to clean out his sink. The cleaner was in a margarine tub. I took the tub and turned to take it to the dumpster. As I turned, I came face to face with the warden, an older man who was not liked by the guards, administrators, or prisoners.

He threateningly asked me what I had in my hand. I told him that it was cleaner that I was going to throw away. He told me that I was wrong. He stated that the prisoner never should have had the cleaning compound in the first place, and therefore it was contraband. Because I took it from the prisoner, I was in possession of contraband and therefore would receive a ticket for possession. The warden explained the scenario to a guard and told him to write me a ticket. It was then that I informed the warden that in fact I had been disposing of contraband all morning pursuant to his direct orders. He thought about that for a while, looked angrily at the guard, and told him to forget it. I then disposed of the cleaner.

•   •   •

The most important document for an inmate is the pre-sentence investigation report, or PSI. As a practicing attorney, I recalled my clients receiving the report on the day they were sentenced. The sentence is based primarily on the factual information placed in that report. I would bring them the PSI as they awaited sentencing in the holding cell. I always advised my clients to check the report for any deletions, additions, or mistakes. On occasion, a client would find a mistake, and it would be noted on the court record. The judge would order that the report be amended to conform to the record, but that wasn't always done. Once my client was sentenced, my job was finished. What many attorneys do not understand is that once that document becomes part of the inmate's personal file, every word in it is deemed to be true until the document is changed by the sentencing court.

I met an individual in prison who had been sentenced to one to five years for felony drunk driving. As his first year was coming to an end, he went before the parole board. His parole was denied because there was also a charge of felonious assault on his PSI. At the time of his sentencing, he had told his attorney the information on the PSI relating to an assault was incorrect. The attorney told the sentencing judge, and the judge assured everyone he would not consider the assault for purposes of sentencing. Unfortunately, no one had the information removed from the PSI, and the parole board refused to listen to the explanation given by the inmate. I informed him that he would have to contact the attorney who had handled his case and have the PSI amended to remove the assault from his file. This matter took some time to complete, but the inmate was granted an expedited hearing and finally was granted his parole—six months later.

• • •

It was my five-month anniversary of being sentenced, November 18, at 7:15 P.M. I was in my cell writing a letter to my family when I heard what sounded like an explosion. I stayed in my cell until I saw others going out and standing on the catwalk. There are five tiers of cells facing each other, and I was on the third tier. As I got to the railing and looked down, the first thing I noticed was that the pool table was absolutely destroyed. An inmate had jumped from the fourth tier and landed on the table. Because the table featured slate on top of plywood, there was some give, and the table partially broke his fall. The inmate was still conscious when the correctional officers put him in a wheelchair and rushed him out of the cell block. I heard a week later that he had died.

Many of the inmates on the various tiers were running back and forth, yelling and laughing at what they had just witnessed. What could have been going through their minds?

What despair the jumper must have felt. He had been down on base (the main floor) earlier in the night and gave no indication of what was to come. Perhaps his parole had been turned down. Perhaps he had been abandoned by his family, as many are. Perhaps the weight of his crime pulled him over the railing.

Whom do we pity more? The jumper or those who found some form of entertainment in this most tragic of acts?

•   •   •

While I was in quarantine, my brother sent me *Harry Potter and the Sorcerer's Stone*. I could not for the life of me understand why he would send me a children's book. I soon found out. It was wonderful—impossible to put down. I read the other books in the series as well and enjoyed many hours at Hogwarts. I introduced a number of people at Jackson Prison to Harry Potter. Every time an individual would read the first book, he would finish the series.

I specifically recall an evening when a young man came to my cell. He said, "Mr. Burke, I hear you have books you let people read." I explained that my family had sent me a large number of books and that I would be happy to let him read any of them. I then suggested the Harry Potter series, and he just laughed, saying he wasn't interested in children's books. I made a deal with him. If he would agree to read the first fifty pages of *The Sorcerer's Stone*, I would give him as many books as he wanted. He agreed.

The next afternoon he returned to tell me he was halfway through the book, and it was the best thing he had ever read. He finished the series within days, and we had many discussions about those books. I told him that I had requested a "Nimbus

2000" for Christmas that year, its use in prison being self-evident. Two people may have never been more different, but for that short period of time, we became friends because of Harry Potter.

• • •

I spent time helping other inmates compose letters to their families or assisting with letters regarding legal issues. Over time, many people came to appreciate that I was willing to help without expecting or accepting any type of payment in return. One afternoon, when I was standing in line waiting to use the microwave to boil water for my coffee, the young black man who was standing in front of me said, "Go ahead, OG; you can warm up your water." Although I appreciated that he let me go in front of him, it bothered me that he would refer to me as OG or the old guy. I later was told by another inmate that OG was actually a term of respect and stood for Original Gangster. I still sign family e-mails "og371292."

• • •

Inmates at Parnell are allowed eight visits a month, but most have no visitors. I, fortunately, received the maximum amount allowed every month. I do not understand how people survive the horror of prison without ever having visits.

Some visits are with people who never knew the prisoner before he was incarcerated. This occurs most often when a prisoner knows of a woman on the outside who would like to correspond. After the two spend a short time exchanging letters, this may ripen into an in-person visit. There are quite a few visits of this nature.

Visits are strictly regulated by the department of corrections because of the tremendous potential for abuse. The primary concern is the introduction of contraband into the system. Because visitors are a primary source of drugs, money, and other contraband for prisoners, they are searched before they visit. Even though the prisoners are strip-searched after visits to make sure no contraband makes its way into the system, it still does. Anything can be purchased in prison.

Nothing could ever bring me more joy than a visit from my family. At the same time, the most troubling experiences I had in prison were watching my wife and daughters being searched before they were allowed to visit. I could see the looks on their faces as they were patted down by prison personnel. As soon as they came in to greet me, I could forget entirely where I was and simply enjoy spending time with them, but as I lay in my bed after those visits, I couldn't get the picture of them being searched out of my mind.

The closest I ever came to getting in a fight was the result of a visit. I was sitting in the dining hall having dinner when an announcement came over the speaker that there was a visit for Michael Burke. I immediately gathered up my tray and hurried to drop it off so I could go out to the visiting room. In my haste, I bumped into someone standing in line waiting to drop off his own tray. He was huge. He turned around and before I could apologize, he said, "What the fuck is wrong with you?" My heart was pounding and I was terrified. I put my head down and said nothing. His voice boomed again, "What the fuck is wrong with you?" I kept my head down. I knew if I looked him in the eyes, it would all be over. He left the dining hall first, and I gave him several minutes to get out of sight. I left and turned to go to my visit. I was sick to my stomach all night. The fear I had experienced was unbearable.

● ● ●

There always has been some form of currency in a prison setting and there always will be. Currency is necessary for buying things on the yard and for the number-one prison pastime, gambling. When I first arrived in prison, the currency was stamps. In an effort to do away with that currency, the administration would allow the purchase of stamps that were already affixed to envelopes. Near the time of my release from prison, the currency had evolved to a bar of soap. It was not unusual to see an inmate in the yard with a pillowcase full of soap to pay off his wagers after a bad day of betting on professional football.

The store man is a necessary part of the prison population. He is the entrepreneur. Each inmate is entitled to buy personal goods from the prison store on a weekly basis. For whatever reason, there is always someone who depletes his goods before the week is over or is unable to purchase goods through the prison store. These people can purchase what they want from the store man at an inflated cost. In reality, this assures that most people can have goods when they want if they are able to pay for them. The official position of the prison administration is that these sales are not to be condoned, but it is a rare occasion when correctional officers bother the store man.

•   •   •

One day, I was coming back from the dining hall when a young inmate I knew informed me that while I was at dinner, he had seen another inmate in my cell. The cell doors were supposed to be locked with a combination lock when the occupant was somewhere else, but I had made a habit of false-locking my cell because it was difficult for me to see the numbers without my reading glasses. The lock had the appearance of being locked but was not snapped shut. The young man informed me that after everyone had left the cell block for dinner, he witnessed the inmate enter my cell and remove some items. Going in another inmate's cell for any reason is a major violation and can result in further criminal charges being brought against the inmate who does it.

That particular day had been store day, and I had left my purchases in a bag on my bed when I went to dinner. On returning to my cell, I discovered that not only had my store purchases been taken, but my radio and a few other personal items also were missing.

I knew who the inmate was. He had stopped by my cell on a number of occasions, seeking a shot of coffee. Most inmates would charge other inmates two shots of coffee for each shot given. I only asked that he return the shot I gave him. I was surprised that this particular individual had broken into my cell and stolen my goods. It did not take long for the word to circulate around the yard that I had been robbed.

While looking for the inmate, I was confronted by an individual I knew to be the head of the Moabites, a prison sect of Black Muslims. They are composed of two groups: the teachers and the warriors. A dispute with one is a dispute with all of them. The head of this group told me that he knew of many good things I had done on the compound to help members of his sect and that he appreciated my helping other inmates. The person who went in my cell had been a member of this group at one time but had been asked to leave because he had a serious gambling problem and had been stealing to pay his gambling debts. Gambling and stealing were not condoned in the Moabite community. He told me that he would do all in his power to have my property returned.

Within a few days the inmate was transferred to another prison, and I never again saw any of the property he had stolen from me. I accepted this incident as God's way of letting me know what it felt like to have property stolen by a compulsive gambler. I was given a little taste of my own medicine.

•   •   •

My next job assignment was as porter in the visiting room. The job was a nightmare. It consisted of cleaning up the administrative offices before the start of visitation hours, and then sitting in the visitation room during visiting hours, waiting to clean up any messes. After visiting hours were over, we cleaned up the visiting room, the bathroom used by the visitors, and the visitors' waiting room. When we were working, we were not allowed to read books or talk to one another. We had to sit for five hours with nothing to do.

To make matters worse, one of the officers in charge of the visiting room despised me. I never knew what caused those feelings, but they were apparent. We usually started our duties as the visitors began to leave. One night, I was cleaning off tables when one of the correctional officers motioned for me to step out. Once I was in the hall, three officers stood around me and handcuffed me. As I was standing there wondering what in God's name was going on, the officer who disliked me came out of the office, looked me in the eye, and said, "I've got you now, you fucker." Two of the correctional officers removed me from the visiting room and walked me across the yard with my hands cuffed behind my back. There were some inmates still in the yard, and they could not believe what they were seeing. No one explained to me what I was accused of doing, and I said nothing. I was taken into ten block and put in "the hole," the isolation cell. I learned later that I had been accused by the officer who disliked me of striking a ten-year-old child in the visiting room. A charge of that nature could have resulted in having to spend more time in prison. I was terrified. Two days later, I received the formal charges that had been filed against me, and I responded immediately.

I made a request to the hearing officer who was appointed to this case to obtain a copy of the videotapes from the visiting room that night. I knew I had done nothing wrong, but I was no longer sure whether that mattered. I was released from the hole after five days. While I was there, my meals had been brought to the cell, I had been allowed only one shower, no books, and no communication with others. Never in my life had I felt so vulnerable.

When I appeared for my hearing, I was informed that the mother of the young boy had written a letter saying I never struck her son, so the charges were dismissed. When I asked the hearing officer about the videotapes from the visitation room, she told me she asked for the tapes but was told the cameras were not working that particular night. I learned an invaluable lesson that day. If they want to get you, they can. There is nothing you can do about it. That was by far the most terrifying week I spent in prison.

•　•　•

During this period of time, I still was attempting to get into good enough physical shape for boot camp. All my life I hated running. It took one and a half years of training to work up the stamina to run two miles consistently. This had been a significant personal achievement, and I could hardly wait to inform my doctor that I now was ready for boot camp. He seemed as excited as I was. The only thing remaining between me and boot camp was a battery of blood work. Within a month of having the blood drawn, I was back in my doctor's office. He informed me that based on the blood work, my application was denied. My iron was well below acceptable standards. He said my iron deficiency could be attributable directly to my vegetarian diet. It would take four months of eating meat and taking supplements to return my iron count to an acceptable level.

Finally, after two long years, I received medical clearance to attend boot camp. A few weeks later, I received the highly anticipated letter from the boot camp administrator. It simply said that my application was denied. No reason for that denial was ever given.

Looking back on that entire episode, I guess I am happy about the way it finally was resolved. I am not at all sure I could have survived the physical rigors demanded of the boot camp participants. However, I am sure that my physical health would not be what it is today had it not been for my efforts to participate, and I know that those first two years passed more quickly because I was working toward that goal.

• • •

My third year in prison I was eligible for my first parole hearing. Three members of the parole board review the inmate's record, and one member actually comes to the prison to interview the applicant. After the interview, a decision is made by the board to either grant or deny the parole. A written notice of the determination comes about four weeks after the hearing. I had been a model inmate, so there was no reason in the world that I should not have been granted a parole—but I also knew that did not always matter. If the board wanted to deny my parole, I would be "flopped" and have to wait another year for my next hearing.

When the time arrived for my response to come in the mail, the stress was intense. On the day it arrived from the board, I went back to my bunk and waited to open it until I was sure no one was near.

My parole had been granted, and I would be allowed to go home after spending two years and eight months in prison.

• • •

My last night I lay awake in my bunk, unable to close my eyes, wondering what the next day would bring. There was a part of me that was terrified something would happen to delay my release.

In the morning, a prison van picked me up and drove me to the building where the processing of the paperwork would be completed. I was one of twenty-five being released that morning. The correctional officer called one inmate at a time. After the paperwork was completed, the inmate was given civilian clothes. The majority of the inmates then would wait for the prison van to drive them to the bus depot in the city so they could start their journey home.

As I awaited my turn, I watched as another inmate was called for processing. The correctional officer told him that his paperwork was incomplete and that he would have to return to his cell block. Decisions like this cannot be questioned. The inmate must return to his cell and attempt to have the paperwork completed in a manner that conforms to what has been mandated. Witnessing that caused my heart to pound even harder. I was sure someone would find a mistake in my own paperwork.

But my processing went through without incident. I was dressed in a few minutes and raced up the stairs, where I was greeted by my family. I ran to the nearest bathroom to put on the clothes my wife had brought, wanting to leave the last remnants of prison life behind me. I threw the prison-issued clothes into the garbage and started for home.

My Daughters 7

Victim Quote:
"Pathological gambling is a problem which causes
great devastation to many families including my own."
Jane Burke

People who are active in their addictions are incapable of understanding the effect their actions are going to have on the ones they love. Our daughters were raised in a safe and loving environment. Both were excellent students and deeply committed to extracurricular activities.

Jane and I had been married eleven years before our first daughter was born, and we both realized that the joys our children provided on a daily basis far exceeded anything else life had to offer. We were fortunate because our jobs allowed us to participate in many of their activities. These were some of the happiest times that my wife and I had ever had. Both of our careers were going well, the girls were a constant source of pleasure, and my relationship with my wife was extraordinary. I thought I had it all.

However, the sad fact is the power my addiction had over me eventually grew greater than my love for my family. It took years for the addiction to take control, but it was too late to do anything about it until a crisis occurred. When the day arrived that I first accepted that I had a problem, my life as I desired it already was over; I was entangled in a web of addiction with no visible signs of escape. As addicts attempt to extricate themselves from their addictions, the guilt and remorse surrounding the pain inflicted upon loved ones is almost more than they can bear; in fact, some cannot bear it.

My daughters offered to share their stories because they feel they have an important message for other families going through what they have survived. The purpose of including these stories is to offer hope for other families who are attempting to deal with the devastation left in the wake of the compulsive gambler. They tell about the betrayal, the loss of trust, and the tremendous impact compulsive gambling had on their lives. Their stories also describe how, over time, we were able to deal with these issues as a family, and even in some ways, have been drawn closer together. The following are the stories of two victims of my addiction: my remarkable daughters.

Amy's Story

On the night of March 30, 2001, I rushed to finish my senior thesis in linguistics at the University of Michigan. It was Friday night, and I was leaving that Sunday for a conference presentation in Tunisia for which I had secured funding through academic grants. I also had a ballet performance the next afternoon with a small group in a community arts festival.

As I was passing by a bank of public phones on my way to the computer lab, I stopped to call home. I never called my family that late at night, and I would see them at the perormance the next day, but I somehow knew I had to speak to them that night. My mother's voice was almost unrecognizable. She assumed that I had gotten the messages she had left for me, but I hadn't been to my apartment since early that morning. Her tone was hollow and unwavering as she asked if I would rather have someone pick me up at Angel Hall or at my apartment; I needed to come home.

I knew that something horrible had happened. I don't remember walking back across campus, but when I heard the messages my family had left for me that day, I began to grasp the extent of the tragedy. The last message was from my sister, disjointed by sobs, asking me to call her as soon as I could. She told me that nothing would ever be the same; she couldn't stand to be at home after what had happened; we had been lied to for years. "He even tried to kill himself," she cried.

The Michigan spring night was silent and freezing cold. I had to do something, to move, so I went outside to get the mail. There were bills, flyers, and a thin envelope from University College London, my first choice for a graduate program. Without any of the emotion I otherwise would have infused into the opening of that envelope, I ripped open the seal and stared at the letter—it was a notice of acceptance. For the next several minutes, I was numb. The seemingly monumental events that I had anticipated for years were entirely overshadowed by a tragedy that I could not begin to comprehend.

My dad's black Cadillac pulled into the driveway. My uncle was driving, my dad in the back seat. I sat with him and held his hand on the drive home as he told me that he had a gambling problem, and that he had lost everything: my parents' savings, their house, our college fund, and even his clients' trust funds. He had turned himself in to the Bar and the local authorities, and he didn't know what would happen next.

I had been worried about my dad's health for several years. I attributed most of the gradual physical and mental changes I noticed to the fact that he was getting older and continued to work long hours. He seemed exhausted and withdrawn, but his familiar humor, warmth, and optimism remained. The only times I saw him angry were when the subject of our family's finances arose. He adamantly refused to participate in any conversation about money, and I thought it was because he felt that he should be trusted to handle his finances as he pleased. That seemed logical to me; we lived comfortably and enjoyed certain luxuries, and both of my parents made a good living.

Throughout my childhood, my dad was the happiest and most generous person I knew. He could make anyone laugh. Every morning before school, when I would reluctantly drag myself out of bed before dawn, I was greeted with a very loud, slightly out-of-tune, improvised song as I came downstairs. When we attended community festivals and school events, he would stop and talk to everyone. I came to know several of the people he had helped over the years, and his willingness to give freely of himself clearly comes from a genuine compassion for his family, friends, and community.

As time went on, I avoided talking about money; the subject arose only twice in the final years of what I later learned was my dad's struggle with compulsive gambling. The first was when I was applying to college in 1997. I had been accepted to the University of Chicago. On a weekend visit to the campus, I went to the financial aid office to learn whether I would be eligible for scholarships or other assistance. The advisor told me that my federal student aid paperwork had never been processed. When I got home, my dad told me that his secretary had mailed it in months ago. I asked for a copy to send to Chicago, and he became furious. He told me that I should be thrilled to go to the University of Michigan, and that spending $120,000 on an undergraduate education was ludicrous. His argument was persuasive, and after getting over my initial indignation, I realized that I had very little about which to complain. My parents had established a college fund for both my sister and me that would pay for in-state tuition and living expenses. I was very lucky to have it.

For the next three years, my tuition and most of my expenses were paid from the college fund. I worked part time to start becoming more independent, but I only earned enough to supplement my living expenses. The fall of my junior year, I was registering for classes for the next semester, and my request was denied because my tuition had not been paid. I knew that my dad paid the university from the college fund, so I called him to ask what had happened. He apologized and told me that he had forgotten to write the check, and he asked me not to mention it to anyone because he was embarrassed for being so absentminded. Two hours later, he came to my door with $3,000 in $100 bills. Why had he not written a check instead? Clearly agitated, he told me that he had been paid by a client in cash and he wanted to get me the money as soon as possible. It wasn't until he had revealed that he was a compulsive gambler that I learned that he had been withdrawing money from the college fund to support his trips to the casino, and that the day he came to my door with cash, he had to borrow it from a family friend.

My initial reaction to the exposure of my dad's addiction was concern for him. As the details of his elaborate system of deception unfolded, I questioned whether I really knew him at all. Each time, I came to the same conclusion. I know that he is an addict, that compulsive gambling is an addiction, and that the devastation he brought on himself, his family, and his victims is the direct result. My immediate and extended family has seen its fair share of addiction and suffered its consequences. That deepened the loss we felt in some ways. Despite the great strides my dad made in his fight against addiction with alcohol, he had fallen prey to an addiction once again, yet addiction is far from the defining feature of my dad.

The weeks, months, and years following the day he came to terms with his gambling proved that my family would never be the same. My family encouraged me to go to Tunisia, so I did. While I was there, my dad underwent emergency triple-bypass surgery. I never would have decided to go if I knew the physical pain he had been enduring for years without seeking medical attention. The local press seized my dad's story, which made my mom and my sister part of a media spectacle while they were trying to deal with their loss. When my sister Katey went to college, my mom had to live alone for the first time in her life, and she struggled to pay for Katey's education. I secured student loans and left for graduate school that fall, but no amount of space or change of environment dulled the feeling of helplessness or concern for my family. I was desperately homesick for the first time, and I anxiously awaited letters from my dad on prison stationery; the only way I could talk to him was when I visited Jackson on my trips home. Every aspect of the prison visits was excruciating except the time we were able to spend with my dad in the visitors' room. His fragile physical state was even more pronounced in his blue prison jumpsuit. I rarely had seen my dad in anything but a suit, and in a mere three months, he lost fifty pounds. He often had scrapes and bruises on his head from thrashing in his sleep while he had nightmares. Once, he fell from his bed and suffered a deep gash that, of course, had been given no medical attention. On the hour drive home to Howell from Jackson, I was left with a sense of despair.

As difficult as those years were, the most important things about our family did not change. My mom remained an unyielding advocate for my sister, my dad, and me; she showed even more tenacity and resolve than she had before my dad went to prison. She began her thirty-fourth year of teaching special education in the community where she and my dad were raised, and she continued to inspire and empower her students and their families. My sister became a caretaker for my entire family, reminding us that the best way to overcome hardship was with each other's support. She remained involved in school activities and emanated maturity and wisdom well beyond her years. My dad began recovering physically and psychologically while he was in prison and started to learn about gambling addiction. He helped other inmates write letters to their families, he loaned them books (but only if they agreed to read a little Harry Potter first), and he earned the respect of guards and fellow inmates alike. I embraced what I had always known to be true—that my family is invaluable and indestructible. My mother's diligence, my sister's compassion, and my father's ability to overcome any obstacle with dignity and optimism truly are remarkable.

For me, the night of March 30, 2001, was when I became aware of just how much my family means to me. Through emergency surgery, harsh sentencing, prison visits, the fear of losing our family home, and financial strain, we became a stronger family. I am proud to be a part of it.

Katey's Story

As a junior in high school, my attention that night was set on one thing: my first prom. I ran into my house excited to tell my parents that I had found the perfect dress. It was long with black sequins, and everything about it was amazing. It cost a lot, so I knew I had to do a good job of convincing them of how important it was to have this great dress. I was never spoiled, but I knew my mom and dad would be in support of this pricey purchase. They loved to see me happy, and they knew how excited I was about the prom. What a wonderful day!

My parents were busily cooking, not paying much attention to what I was saying. They were moving like robots, as if they weren't in control of their own bodies. I asked if something was wrong, and began to wonder if they were angry, because I simply assumed I was going to get the dress. My mom then told me that my aunt and uncle were on the way. She said it like I should have thought it was normal and should not question their visit. It was not normal! They lived two hours away and although they were extremely close to our family, they would never just stop by. I questioned them repeatedly until they both seemed quite annoyed. My dad is never angry, and at this moment, he was more than angry. He told me to leave it alone and walked out of the room. This was not like him; something was wrong, and I knew what it was—my aunt was sick and I knew it was bad. I sat and prepared myself for the news and planned what I would say to comfort her after her sickness was revealed.

I felt sick to my stomach when my aunt and uncle walked into my house. Both of them had red, puffy eyes from crying. My heart was beating faster by the minute. I did not want her to be sick, not now, not ever. We all walked into the living room and sat down. We were sitting so we could see each other in different parts of the room, and for a while, we just stared at one another. Finally, my mom looked directly into my eyes and said, "It's not your aunt, Katey. It's your dad and he's very sick."

For some reason, I knew he was not physically sick. I could feel that it was something he had done. My mom looked at my dad differently than ever before. She had a look of hurt on her face that I had never seen. My dad finally announced that for the past five years he had been suffering from a gambling addiction, and everything was gone. "They found out," he said under his breath. As the words sank in, the tears were streaming down my face. I had no control; I had never cried so hard in my life.

My dad had always been close to perfect in my eyes. He was a successful attorney, he was involved with the schools and many committees, and most importantly, he was an amazing dad. He thought of his family before himself. The only nice things he'd buy were for others, and his own needs always were set aside. How could the best person I know have done such a horrible thing?

As he continued his story, it only got worse. He'd gotten into a bad situation and out of fear, he started to embezzle money from his clients. Over the years, it had added up to more than $1 million. The police knew, and it was going to be in the papers the upcoming week. The words kept coming and I started to fade away. I never knew that emotional pain could cause such an intense physical reaction. I will never forget the way I felt at that moment; I pray I never will feel it again.

In a moment, in a matter of minutes, my life changed. Seventeen years seemed to lead to this instant. I looked at my father and did not recognize him. He was a stranger who had spun an elaborate web of lies. I never lied to my parents. Our family was built on respect and trust. Why would he break our perfect life into pieces? I could not breathe or speak, so I sat and cried. When I composed myself, I said the most hurtful thing I could. I looked at my mom and asked, "Are you going to let this MAN stay in our house?" She simply said, "Katey, I don't know what to do."

My mom did not shed a tear. She sat and spoke as though she was programmed with the right thing to say. Her reaction scared me, and I would rather she had been screaming than be so calm. I later learned that she was in shock. She said all she cared about was my sister and me. I suppose it was a "mom reaction." She dealt with her own feelings weeks, months, and years after the news was revealed.

I initiated a few more interactions with my dad. I can't even remember what I said, but I know nothing he could have said would have made a difference to me. I stood up and felt so dizzy I almost fell back into my chair. I ran into my room as if I was being chased—but there was no person chasing me. I was running from the words, the story, and the reality of my new life. My room had happy pictures of friends and family covering the walls. They seemed to be spinning around, screaming that my life as I knew it was over. I wanted to wake up from the nightmare.

My aunt and uncle met me in my room. They picked me up off the floor and hugged me. All they said was, "Everything will be OK; we promise." I felt so much comfort from them and I knew why my mom felt that it was so important for them to be there. My boyfriend, whom I'd been dating for five years, was knocking at the door to take me to his house. When I got there, his mom brought me a paper bag to breathe into, because she thought I was going to faint. Within an hour, I had five of my closest friends there as well. They were holding my hand, crying with me, and reassuring me that they would be there through it all. At my very worst moment, I could not believe how lucky I was to have these people in my life.

I will never forget that night when everything changed. I thought I was at my lowest point, but it got worse before it got better. Five days later, my dad suffered a massive heart attack and had triple bypass surgery. What timing! The night before his operation, I went to his hospital room. I forgave him and begged him to fight. I said that it was his job to make things right again, and made him promise me that he would. He always had been an amazing dad; now it was my turn to be an amazing daughter.

For the two weeks my dad was recovering, my mom, aunt, sister, and I hid from the news cameras, phone calls, and the overwhelming attention. The media thrived on the downfall of this perfect man with his perfect family in his perfect life. I quickly grew thicker skin and learned to defend my family and myself. Every penny my father took went to the casino. No fancy things were bought for himself or his family; the money was used to feed a fierce addiction. We all studied gambling addictions and when we realized that he was sick—not some vicious monster—we were able to defend him. We, along with many others, were the victims of his addiction. What he did was wrong, but I prayed he still would be given the chance to get the help he needed so he could start to make things right.

My father was sentenced to three years in prison. I went from having a father who was an attorney everyone knew to having a father who was an inmate in Jackson Prison. I went on to lead my varsity pom squad, graduate from high school, and leave home for college. My dad would have been in the front row for it all, like he always had been. Instead, he stayed updated through pictures and letters. I missed him and hoped for his safety every day he was gone. He was released on January 22, 2004. He now gives public talks about his story and the responses he gets show that he is still helping and inspiring others, just as he did for so many years. His goal is to spread the word about gambling addiction so he can stop others from going through what he did. Just last week, he read a note from a man that said, "You saved my life." Those notes are proof that he is doing something right. He will pay his debt to his victims, our community, and our family for the rest of his life.

I would not take back a second of what I've been through. I don't know who I would be without this experience, because I have been able to live my life on each end of the spectrum. I have sat in the most beautiful restaurants around the world with prestigious people, and I have sat in a waiting room of a prison with people who at one point I would have judged, but who now were no different than me. I have learned not to judge people before I know them, because each person has a unique story. This lesson is one that I will carry with me for the rest of my life. Even now when I tell this story, it does not seem real. I am thankful that my life was changed, because it has made me strong, preparing me for whatever is to come.

Life After Prison

8

Judge Quote:
"And I think a very important factor in this case is the fact that I don't believe in my view there's any likelihood of Mr. Burke ever making any substantial payments towards restitution in this case."

My first six months at home were spent getting my feet on the ground, becoming reacquainted with my family, and looking into employment possibilities. I made contacts with some old friends in the legal community to see if there was any opportunity of work associated with the practice of law, but I discovered early on that this was not going to happen. I was a thief and a convicted felon who had spent three years in prison. No one could risk bringing me into a practice.

There could not have been a worse time to look for employment. The entire state of Michigan was in an economic downturn as manufacturing jobs were leaving at an alarming rate. The outlook was bleak even for those people not burdened with a prison number.

The first call I received from someone interested in helping me was Dr. John Franklin, head of addiction studies at the University of Detroit Mercy. John had been a counselor at Brighton Hospital in 1977, and we remained friends since that time. I told him that while I had been in prison, my wife and other family members sent me numerous books and other literature dealing with compulsive gambling, and I was becoming extremely knowledgeable in the field. He felt I should use that expertise and my past experiences to assist other people who are suffering from gambling problems. He offered to have me participate in some joint presentations on compulsive gambling at different venues around the state.

After a few of these talks, he arranged for me to give a solo presentation to the staff at Brighton Hospital. Although I was not aware of it at the time, this actually was my employment interview. As a result of that presentation, I was hired to do a weekly lecture on compulsive gambling. Many of the patients coming into the hospital for substance abuse treatment also were having problems with gambling. Over the next several years, I talked to over 5,000 patients at the hospital. At the end of each presentation, the patients fill out a screening questionnaire for gambling. Sixteen percent of those patients identify as a problem/compulsive gambler. This number seems to be representative of similar studies.

What is most interesting about my findings is they show that of the 84 percent who did not identify as having a problem with gambling, the majority do not gamble. This is contrary to studies that show a large percentage of the general population gambles in some limited capacity. The obvious question is this: Why is this particular group of people different from the general population?

About one year into my talks and reviewing surveys, the answer came to me: *There was no need to get involved in an additional addictive behavior because the addiction that brought them to treatment in the first place was working just fine.* Their present addiction consumed every moment of their lives to the exclusion of all else. There simply was no time or desire for gambling. Unfortunately, for some in this group, like me, a gambling problem would start after they left treatment and successfully learned how to deal with their substance abuse. Most start gambling for entertainment only and are not aware that this activity can become addicting. It can take years for gambling to mutate from a purely recreational experience to the life-destroying addiction known as compulsive gambling. This transformation can be difficult to define, and in many cases when it is finally apparent that an individual has a problem, that person already has crossed the line into compulsive gambling. The people in this particular group need to be given factual information about compulsive gambling so that they can make an informed choice before they ever get started gambling.

My experiences at Brighton Hospital have taught me how important it is to get this message to those in the recovering community. I spend a great deal of my time warning these individuals that they must stay away from *all* forms of gambling. For them, a trip to the casino or the purchase of a lottery ticket can be as dangerous as snorting cocaine. They may not become addicted to either one the first few times they do it, but eventually either one will exact its toll.

Most of the people I've talked with who have developed a gambling problem had no idea how deeply they had become involved in gambling until it was too late. Many led productive and exemplary lives and had been strong contributors to their communities. Their families had taken pride in their accomplishments. In order to support their addiction, many became involved in activities that would have been unthinkable before the gambling took over. Many proponents of gambling refer to these tales of destruction as *anecdotal stories*. This is perhaps the greatest insult of all—an attempt to minimize the devastation suffered by another human being so the bottom line will not be affected. People whose lives have been destroyed by gambling are looked upon by the gambling industry and the states that rely on gambling revenues as *collateral damage*. Over the last few years, I have had the opportunity to speak to many of these people whose lives have been devastated by gambling. Unfortunately, by the time they get to me, everything usually is gone. Savings accounts are wiped out, credit cards are maxed out, checks have bounced, money has been borrowed from friends, and retirement accounts have been decimated, all in an effort to satisfy this insatiable beast known as compulsive gambling.

Two other groups that seem to be predisposed to gambling problems are teenagers and senior citizens, and I have worked with both over the past several years. Teenagers present a unique set of problems. Most have to steal from their families to obtain gambling funds. Many of the young people I have worked with are extremely intelligent and, like most teens, feel they are indestructible. These kids are drawn to the new Texas Hold 'Em craze that they see on television and play on their computers whenever they wish. I have talked to high school students who travel around the county during the school day to play cards. Sometimes these kids will go to the homes where the games are played and not know one other person who is playing. They seem so surprised when they leave a few hours later and all their money is gone. Many have told me their desire is to drop out of school and become professional gamblers. Several have devastated their families financially, but still insist they "know" they can make a living playing poker.

Most feel that their only reason for losing was that they did not possess a big enough bankroll when they started. If they only had a little more money, their system would have worked. Over the last several years, I have had a number of teenagers sent to me by lawyers, counselors, and families. I try to get through to them, but they often leave with a look that tells me they know that what has happened to other people with gambling problems will never happen to them because they are different.

The other age group I am heavily involved with is senior citizens. Several years ago, I gave my presentation to a local Lions club. After the talk, a gentleman in his seventies asked if he could speak with me. He told me that his wife of fifty years had passed away a little more than a year ago. Since her death, he found himself going to the casinos on a regular basis and playing the slot machines. He had lost a tremendous sum of money in the last year. He now understood that gambling was how he was coping with the loss of his wife, and he said it sickened him that this was how he was honoring her memory. He told me he would never go to the casino again, and thanked me for my presentation.

One of the most disturbing stories I have read about casino gambling is that casinos in Atlantic City, New Jersey, have become day care for the elderly. Most casinos offer bus rides to seniors and hand out "free" lunch vouchers. Many seniors spend their Social Security checks and their retirement income at the casinos. If this is the best that we as a nation can do for our senior citizens, then we should be ashamed.

In addition to speaking to groups and individuals, much of the last two years has been spent writing this book. The purpose is twofold. The first is to disseminate information to the compulsive gambler and the families and friends of the compulsive gambler. I remember when I went through my downfall that there was little information to help my family and me understand why and how we were suffering. It is my sincere hope that some people who are in as much pain as I was might find some comfort and hope in knowing that they can come through positively from this addiction.

The second is a desire to repay some part of the $1.6 million to my victims. The likelihood of my ever obtaining meaningful employment seems doubtful. Writing is something I could do that holds out the possibility of making some restitution. When I was in prison, I remember that the other inmates could not believe that I had lost all my money gambling; no attorney could ever be that stupid. They were convinced that when I got out of jail, I simply would go out in the backyard, dig it up, and live in the lap of luxury.

Life has been quite different from that. I am dependent on my wife for my necessities. My stipend from Brighton Hospital allows only enough for gas money so I can speak to various groups. I have no savings. I have no credit cards. I have no bank accounts. I own nothing. My purpose in life today is to warn as many people as I can of the dangers of compulsive gambling. I find it to be a noble purpose that has given meaning to a life once stripped of any meaning.

I normally end my presentations, and will end this chapter, by informing my audience: "I will never use my addiction as an excuse for what I did, only as an explanation for what has happened."

Identification of the Compulsive Gambler

9

"The unit of survival [or adaptation] is organism plus environment.
We are learning by bitter experience that the organism which destroys its environment destroys itself."
Gregory Bateson, British anthropologist

Gambling is going to continue its growth at an explosive rate. As of February 2008, legislation passed in Missouri, allowing four new casinos to open in Kansas City and to be operated by the state. Thus, Missouri becomes the first state to operate a casino. This should send a strong message to the thirty-eight states now offering lotteries that there is a new way for the states to relieve their citizens of their entertainment dollars and add significantly to state revenues. No longer will the states have to settle for simply the tax dollars; now they can have it all. It is a perfect monopoly: The states can create it, run it, and even regulate their own industry. The fox is not just in the henhouse—he owns it!

Legalized gambling is available everywhere. Local bars and convenience stores have electronic gaming devices; several states offer a multitude of different lottery games including the Mega Millions, Power Ball, and Fantasy 5. It is possible to go into a grocery store and find at least twenty-five different scratch-off game tickets. A variety of casinos, both tribal and commercial, have opened around the country. Most states find it necessary to "sanitize" the revenues they receive from gambling. Instead of adding these monies to the general fund, they often are earmarked for causes such as education. The state then has extra money in the general fund because less has to be spent on the cause, in this case, education. When a state announces its gambling revenues are going for the benefit of children, it is simply disingenuous.

Today, there seems to be a general acceptance that a segment of society suffers from a medically defined condition known as problem/compulsive gambling.

> Pathological gambling is a chronic and progressive failure to resist impulses to gamble, and gambling behavior that compromises, disrupts, or damages personal, family or vocational pursuits. The gambling preoccupation, urge and activity increase during periods of stress. Problems that arise as a result of the gambling lead to an intensification of the gambling behavior. Characteristic problems include extensive indebtedness and consequent default on debts and other financial responsibilities, disrupted family relationships, inattention to work, and financially motivated illegal activities to pay for gambling.[1]

Studies confirm a correlation between the population's proximity to casinos and an increase in the number of compulsive gamblers.[2] The greater the number of gambling opportunities offered, the greater the numbers of people directly and indirectly affected by problem gambling.

In 1964, New Hampshire became the first state to sponsor a lottery. In 1978, New Jersey followed Nevada to become the second state to legalize casino gambling. By 2007, only Hawaii and Utah did not offer some form of legalized gambling. In 1997, the number of people who suffered from problem/pathological gambling was estimated to be between 7 and 15 million nationally.[3] In the last forty-plus years, gambling has gone from being an immoral and illegal activity allowed in one state to an activity condoned in most states. This creates a new source of revenue for the governing bodies of those states that find the thought of tax increases synonymous with term limits. Raise taxes, and the tenure of a legislator is terminated by the voters.

The *domino effect* is the most common argument used by politicians who have endorsed legalized gambling as a way to assist in balancing their state budgets. The phrase "domino effect" is used in reference to a state that does not have legalized gambling but adjoins a state that does. The argument goes that the easy accessibility that a state's citizens have to casino gambling gives rise to the belief that the state is exporting gambling dollars while importing and being financially responsible for the social harm resulting from gambling. It is one of the few times that one will ever hear politicians acknowledge that there are social costs associated with gambling.

In 1997, a study was undertaken by the National Gambling Impact Study Commission, resulting in a consensus among the commissioners on two major issues:

1. There is an immediate need to address pathological gambling.
2. It is time to consider a pause in the expansion of gambling.[4]

Unfortunately, as of 2008, neither of those recommendations has been addressed. If anything, there has been an explosion of all forms of legalized gambling since the study was released.

Compulsive gambling is different from most other addictions in that there are no tell-tale signs. Unlike the alcoholic, there is no strong odor of intoxicants, no slurred speech, and no staggering. Gambling historically has been a hidden disease. Many families either have no knowledge that a family member gambles at all, or if they are aware, they are led to believe the gambling is on a much smaller scale than is being admitted.

The gambler lives in a world of lies. The gambler who acknowledges he or she gambles will lie about the time spent gambling and the amount of money lost. Most gamblers will say that they either won money or lost less money than they actually lost. The most difficult reality for gamblers to accept is the simple fact that if they gamble on a regular basis, they must lose. In a scene in the movie *Casino*, the casino manager, played by Robert De Niro, ponders the inability of the compulsive gambler to comprehend the inevitable: "What they don't understand is that in the end we get it all."

For the person who has a predisposition to addiction, the lure of gambling easily can replace an addiction that is in remission. For this reason, people in the addiction-recovery community **must** stay away from any type of gambling. Some studies have shown that over 50 percent of the people who attend Gamblers Anonymous have a history of substance abuse. Addiction is an addiction is an addiction. If the spouse, family member, or friend of a person who is recovering from a substance abuse problem sees that he or she is drawn to gambling, that spouse, friend, or family member needs to pass on the warning about the high probability of trading one addiction for another. Substance abusers should *not* gamble.

Gamblers lie about money. The spouse of a person who gambles must be aware of the family's finances to protect the family. If the gambler has large sums of cash, or if large sums of cash are missing from the family accounts, the spouse must demand details. If a person is in a committed relationship but doesn't know about the flow of money, he or she does not know anything about the relationship. One of the greatest pitfalls for a compulsive gambler is access to money. As the addiction increases, the gambler needs more money to feed his or her habit.

If a spouse acknowledges a gambling problem, get his or her name off all shared accounts. A spouse normally will learn of a gambling problem when funds come up missing, credit cards get maxed out, or checks start bouncing. It is critical to remember that the gambler will find it impossible to tell the whole truth, and he or she normally will preserve one or more lies. It is simply impossible for the gambler to make a complete disclosure. The reason for this is that, more likely than not, there will be relapses, and access by the gambler to funds will be necessary so the gambling can resume. The gambler who is not finished with gambling will attempt to maintain a stash.

The way to protect a family when it becomes apparent that a spouse is a compulsive gambler is to take away all known credit cards and to remove the gambler's name from all savings and checking accounts. Make absolutely sure that there are no joint accounts from which the nongambling spouse can be held liable for the debts of the compulsive gambler. If there is a joint line of credit of any type, have the gambler's name removed. There is no guaranteed way to protect the gambler who is in an addiction, but these suggestions will help protect the nongambling spouse and the rest of the family.

Gambling normally causes a betrayal of trust between the gambler and his or her spouse. If a person discovers that his or her spouse has a gambling problem and he or she decides to stay with the gambler, *demand accountability.* If the gambler is not willing to account for his or her time when the couple is not together, the relationship should end. The gambler has lied for a long time about the depth of the problem and probably has invaded family finances to feed the addiction. This will be the time for constructive action and accountability. The spouse must demand this accountability *at the time the crisis occurs,* because this is the time when the gambler will feel the most shame and be the most likely to agree to any demands. The spouse of the gambler probably should do some checking up on the whereabouts of the gambler, demand an accounting for all monies spent, and participate in the treatment available to the gambler. The gambler must agree to be available at all times to phone contact by the spouse. If the phone is turned off, or the gambler does not pick up, the spouse should be concerned that something is not right. Gamblers do not like to answer their phones inside a casino or when in the midst of any gambling activity. It removes them from their magical world and also could give away their location.

As in any addiction, compulsive gamblers go through phases, and it sometimes is possible to see the beginning of a gambling problem. The three phases of compulsive gambling are winning, losing, and desperation.[5] If a person seems to have a preoccupation with gambling, it could be a precursor of problems to come. This is evident when everything a person does seems to be associated with some type of gambling activity. Another red flag is raised when a person takes time from family or work to gamble. Perhaps there is a family holiday dinner and one member of the family wants to leave the get-together to go to the casino. A very serious sign of a problem is when an individual attempts to conceal gambling, an attempt that makes no sense unless there is a problem.

If a friend or family member needs to borrow money and does not supply a good reason, investigate further to determine if there is a problem with gambling. If the money is being borrowed to gamble or to pay for a problem created by gambling, the individual is at high risk of having a gambling problem. Imagine how difficult it is for that person to come to a friend or relative for the money. It is an act of desperation. However, the next probable step for this individual is to break the law to get money. If a person says that he or she is going to quit or cut back on gambling, this is a very serious sign of a problem. If a person lies to hide the gambling, this person has a problem.

The foundation of any addiction is lies! If any of these just-noted problems are seen, discuss the situation with that person. If a person cares about that person, he or she will be honest. It may be the honesty of the questioner that gets the gambler to deal with the addiction in an appropriate manner. Remember, *20 percent* of all compulsive gamblers attempt suicide.[6] *An honesty inquiry might save a life.*

Many screening tools are available to help identify the compulsive gambler. Three of the most widely us ed are included here. They are the twenty questions from the Gamblers Anonymous *Combo Book*, the screening checklist questions used by mental health professionals from the American Psychological Association's *Diagnostic and Statistical Manual of Mental Disorders,* 4th edition (DSM-IV), and the ten questions of the South Oaks Gambling Screen (SOG). If a person thinks someone has a gambling problem, simply have that person take the test. The answers give an immediate determination disclosing if there is a gambling problem. Also included here is a twenty-question test from Gam-Anon. To question a gambling problem, take this test and determine whether the person cared about does have a problem.

My feeling about this topic is quite simple: If a person thinks that someone has a gambling problem, he or she probably does. If it appears that a spouse, loved one, or friend has a gambling problem, the next step is getting that person some effective treatment.

GAMBLERS ANONYMOUS TWENTY QUESTIONS

1. Did you ever lose time from work or school due to gambling?
2. Has gambling ever made your home life unhappy?
3. Did gambling affect your reputation?
4. Have you ever felt remorse after gambling?
5. Did you ever gamble to get money with which to pay debts or otherwise solve financial difficulties?
6. Did gambling cause a decrease in your ambition or efficiency?
7. After losing did you feel you must return as soon as possible and win back your losses?
8. After a win did you have a strong urge to return and win more?
9. Did you often gamble until your last dollar was gone?
10. Did you ever borrow to finance your gambling?
11. Have you ever sold anything to finance gambling?
12. Were you reluctant to use "gambling money" for normal expenditures?
13. Did gambling make you careless of the welfare of yourself or your family?
14. Did you ever gamble longer than you had planned?

15. Have you ever gambled to escape worry or trouble?
16. Have you ever committed, or considered committing, an illegal act to finance gambling?
17. Did gambling cause you to have difficulty in sleeping?
18. Do arguments, disappointments or frustrations create within you an urge to gamble?
19. Did you ever have an urge to celebrate any good fortune by a few hours of gambling?
20. Have you ever considered self destruction or suicide as a result of your gambling?

Most compulsive gamblers will answer yes to at least seven of these questions.

DSM-IV CHECKLIST

1. Are you preoccupied with gambling (e.g., preoccupied with reliving past gambling experiences, handicapping or planning the next venture, or thinking of ways to get money with which to gamble)?
2. Do you need to gamble with increasing amounts of money in order to achieve the desired excitement?
3. Have you made repeated unsuccessful efforts to control, cut back, or stop gambling?
4. Are you restless or irritable when attempting to cut down or stop gambling?
5. Do you gamble as a way of escaping from problems or of relieving feelings of helplessness, guilt, anxiety, or depression?
6. After losing money gambling, do you often return another day to get even?
7. Do you lie to family members, therapists, or to others to conceal the extent of involvement with gambling?
8. Have you committed illegal acts such as forgery, fraud, theft, or embezzlement to finance gambling?

9. Have you jeopardized or lost a significant relationship, job or educational or career opportunity because of gambling?
10. Do you rely on others to provide money to relieve a desperate financial situation caused by gambling?

THE SOUTH OAKS GAMBLING SCREEN

1. Please indicate which of the following types of gambling you have done in your lifetime. After each type of gambling, answer: "not at all," "less than once a week," or "once a week or more."

    a. play cards for money
    b. bet on horses, dogs or other animals (at OTB, the track or with a bookie)
    c. bet on sports (parlay cards, with a bookie or at Jai Alai)
    d. play dice games (including craps, over and under or other dice games) for money
    e. gamble in a casino (legal or otherwise)
    f. play the numbers or bet on lotteries
    g. play bingo for money
    h. play the stock, options and/or commodities market
    i. play slot machines, poker machines or other gambling machines
    j. bowl, shoot pool, play golf or play any other game of skill for money
    k. pull tabs or "paper" games other than lotteries
    l. engage in some form of gambling not listed above (please specify)

2. What is the largest amount of money you have ever gambled with on any one day?

a. I've never gambled
b. $1 or less
c. more than $1 but less than $10
d. more than $10 but less than $100
e. more than $100 but less than $1,000
f. more than $1,000 but less than $10,000
g. more than $10,000

3. Which of the following people has (or had) a gambling problem?

a. father
b. mother
c. brother or sister
d. spouse or partner
e. child or children
f. grandparent
g. another relative
h. no one in my family has (or had) a gambling problem

4. When you gamble, how often do you return to win back the money you lost?

a. never
b. some of the time (less than half of the times I lost)
c. most of the times I lost
d. every time I lost

5. Have you ever claimed to be winning money while gambling, even though you were actually losing?

a. never
b. yes, less than half of the times I lost
c. yes, most of the time

6. Do you feel like you have ever had a problem with betting money or gambling?

   a. no
   b. yes, in the past, but not now
   c. yes

If you have answered (a) or no to all of the questions above, you do not have a gambling problem.

7. Did you ever gamble more than you intended to?
8. Have people criticized your betting or told you that you had a gambling problem, regardless of whether or not you thought it was true?
9. Have you ever felt guilty about the way you gamble or what happens when you gamble?
10. Have you ever felt like you would like to stop betting money or gambling but you didn't think you could?
11. Have you ever hidden betting slips, lottery tickets, gambling money, I.O.U.s or other signs of betting or gambling from your spouse, children or other important people in your life?
12. Have you ever argued with people you live with over how you handle money?
13. (If you answered yes to question 12) Have money arguments ever centered on your gambling?
14. Have you ever borrowed from someone and not paid them back as a result of your gambling?
15. Have you ever lost time from work (or school) due to betting or gambling?
16. If you borrowed money to gamble or to pay gambling debts, who/where did you borrow from? (answer "yes" or "no" to each question)

    a. from household money?
    b. from your spouse?

    c.   from other relatives or in-laws?

    d.   from banks, loan companies or credit unions?

    e.   from credit cards?

    f.   from loan sharks?

    g.   you cashed in stocks, bonds or other securities?

    h.   you sold personal or family property?

    i.   you borrowed on your checking account?

    j.   you have (had) a credit line with a bookie?

    k.   you have (had) a credit line with a casino?

If you have answered (b) or (c) to questions 4 through 6 or yes to questions 7 through 16, one to four times, then you have some problem with gambling.

GAM-ANON QUESTIONS

1. Do you find yourself constantly bothered by bill collectors?

2. Is the person in question often away from home for long, unexplained periods of time?

3. Does this person ever lose time from work due to gambling?

4. Do you feel that this person cannot be trusted with money?

5. Does the person in question faithfully promise that he or she will stop gambling; beg, plead for another chance, yet gamble again and again?

6. Does this person ever gamble longer than he or she intended to, until the last dollar is gone?

7. Does this person immediately return to gambling to try to recover losses, or to win more?

8. Does this person ever gamble to get money to solve financial difficulties, or have unrealistic expectations that gambling will bring the family material comfort and wealth?

9. Does this person borrow money to gamble with or to pay gambling debts?

10. Has this person's reputation ever suffered due to gambling, even to the extent of committing illegal acts to finance gambling?

11. Have you come to the point of hiding money needed for living expenses, knowing that you and the rest of the family may go without food and clothing if you do not?

12. Do you search this person's clothing or go through his or her wallet when the opportunity presents itself or otherwise check on his or her activities?

13. Do you hide his or her money?

14. Have you noticed a personality change in the gambler as his or her gambling progresses?

15. Does the person in question consistently lie to cover-up or deny his or her gambling activities?

16. Does this person use guilt induction as a method of shifting responsibilities off his or her gambling upon you?

17. Do you attempt to anticipate this person's moods, or try to control his or her life?

18. Does this person ever suffer from remorse or depression due to gambling sometimes to the point of self-destruction?

19. Has the gambling ever brought you to the point of threatening to break up the family unit?

20. Do you feel that your life together is a nightmare?

If you are living with a compulsive gambler, you will answer yes to at least six of the above questions. If you answered yes to at least six of these questions, you may want to go to a Gam-Anon meeting.

NOTES

1. American Psychiatric Association, *Diagnostic and Statistical Manual of Mental Disorders*, 3rd ed. (Washington, DC: American Psychiatric Association, 1980).

2. John Warren Kindt, "The Economic Aspects of Legalized Gambling Activities," *Duke Law Review* 43 (1994): 59.

3. Howard Shaffer et al., *Estimating the Prevalence of Disordered Gambling Behavior in the United States and Canada: A Meta-Analysis* (Washington, DC: National Gambling Impact Study Commission, 1997).

4. National Gambling Impact Study Commission, *Final Report* (Washington, DC: National Gambling Impact Study Commission, 1999), 1–7.

5. Robert Custer and Harry Milt, *When Luck Runs Out* (New York: Grand Central Pub., 1995).

6. National Council on Problem Gambling, *Problem and Pathological Gambling in America: The National Picture,* at 14-15 (January 1997) (Washington, DC: National Gambling Impact Study Commission Final Report, 1999).

Treatment for the Compulsive Gambler

10

Judge Quote:
"In my view he had a gambling addiction. OK, fine, you can still not drive your car over there."

The medical profession is at the point with compulsive gambling today where it was thirty years ago with alcoholism. Most people perceive it as a moral weakness and pay lip service to the medical model. Because the opening of casinos around the country is a recent phenomenon, treatment has not caught up to the problems being caused by the latest wave of gambling to hit the country. As a result, there is very little available in the way of treatment.

One of the conclusions reached by the authors of the National Gambling Impact Study:

> More research on the prevalence and causes of problem and pathological gambling clearly is a priority. For the millions of Americans who confront problem and pathological gambling, treatment may be necessary and should be made readily available. For those in need of such treatment, the gambling industry, government, foundations, and other sources of funding should step forward with long-term, sustained support.[1]

Only a handful of inpatient treatment centers exist around the country for the specific purpose of treating compulsive gambling, which speaks to the very nature of the problem. The compulsive gambler who is seeking help for his or her addiction *has no money*; all has been lost by the time treatment is sought. It is a rare event when the gambler seeks treatment while money still remains. Remember, as long as the gambler has money, the gambler has hope. At this time in history, there is little available in the form of insurance coverage to assist in treatment. Insurance companies have been cutting funds for substance abuse treatment for the past twenty years, and they show no inclination to use treatment funds for inpatient gambling treatment.

One successful inpatient program is Core in Shreveport, Louisiana. This is a thirty- to forty-day inpatient treatment program. It is funded by the state and is free to residents of the state. Nonresidents are charged a fee of approximately $5,200 (as of 2008). The state assesses a fee from the casinos to assist in treatment programs for their residents. The philosophy of the state of Louisiana is remarkably simple. It realizes that a small percentage of people who gamble will become addicted and lose control. These people will need treatment. Therefore, the entity that gains the most benefit—the casinos—should help shoulder the responsibility for this group. How enlightening that a state not often recognized for such forward thinking could come up with the most logical solution to the problem. Let the entities that benefit from gambling be responsible for the problems they create.

Many states have established programs offering counseling sessions to compulsive gamblers at no or at an extremely low cost. Many times, the individual can receive up to ten sessions to assist in understanding what has happened in his or her life and how to deal with it from that point on. Funds for these services usually come from the state and the casinos as an effort to do something about the compulsive gambling problem. Information about these services usually can be obtained by contacting the gambling helpline in the state of residence. In addition, those seeking assistance can contact the National Gambling Helpline at 1-800-522-4700 or visit www.ncpgambling.org.

Possibly the most successful program for a person with a gambling problem is Gamblers Anonymous, patterned after other twelve-step programs. A helpline assists the gambler in finding where the nearest meeting is located. At these meetings, a person with a gambling problem not only gets the chance to talk to others about his or her gambling problems, but also has the opportunity to hear from others who have suffered from the same addiction and found a way to live their lives free of the shackles of compulsive gambling.

The family and friends of the compulsive gambler can find great help and understanding by attending Gam-Anon meetings, where they will find answers to many of their questions. The most difficult concept for a family member to understand is that they could do nothing to keep their loved one from gambling, and that nothing they ever did caused their loved one to gamble. The compulsive gambler gambles because he or she suffers from an addiction.

An extremely small percentage of people suffering from gambling-related issues seek treatment. Much of this has to do with the guilt and shame associated with the gambling addiction. Another major factor has to do with crime. Over 70 percent of compulsive gamblers will commit an illegal act to get money with which to gamble or to pay for problems created by their gambling.[2] Gamblers are warned at the beginning of every Gamblers Anonymous meeting: "It is suggested that members do not discuss any crimes for which they may still be prosecuted, because anonymity is not a legal right, and the room itself offers no protection regarding these matters." Notwithstanding this statement, Gamblers Anonymous remains the primary source of treatment for compulsive gamblers.

The future for treatment is looking more hopeful. A great number of people are coming to understand that the person with a gambling problem who seeks treatment has no money left to pay for that treatment; therefore, some other source for treatment funds must be found. Casinos earn more than half their revenues from problem and pathological gamblers.[3] Five percent of the population that purchases lottery tickets purchase 50 percent of all lottery tickets.[4] The states and the casinos that make billions from legalized gambling are starting to acknowledge their responsibilities and are providing some treatment monies for those who have lost everything. Hopefully, they will follow the path established by Louisiana and offer similar inpatient programs like Core. Gamblers and their families need assistance in obtaining treatment so they can better deal with the devastation left in the wake of their addiction. Who better to bear the costs of these programs than the entities that have benefited the most from the gamblers' losses—the states and the casinos?

NOTES

1. National Gambling Impact Study Commission, *Final Report* (Washington, DC, 1999), 4–19.

2. Valerie Lorenz, "Dear God, Just Let Me Win," *Christian Social Action,* July/August 1994, 26.

3. Earl Grinols, Statement Before U.S. House of Representatives Committee on the Judiciary, September 28, 1995.

4. Charles T. Clotfelter and Philip Cook, *Selling Hope: State Lotteries in America* (Cambridge, MA: Harvard University Press, 1989), 92.

Epilogue

In the past two years, I have been fortunate to give my presentation on compulsive gambling to thousands of people. Groups included compulsive gamblers, families of compulsive gamblers, law schools, the Michigan Bar Association, the American Bar Association, university classes, service organizations, rehabilitation centers, and churches. I am completing this book by offering some of their comments. As I reread them, I am reminded that things happen in our lives for a reason. The challenge is the manner in which we respond to those events.

Appendix A
Comments from Presentations

Dear Mike,

I had the opportunity to listen to your CD at one of my counseling sessions. I recently have been attending these sessions for my gambling addiction. My therapist is Rhonda L. Rhonda is a therapist that specializes in gambling addiction. I was referred to her by calling the 1-800-270-7117 number that was located on the back of my Greek Town/Motor City gaming cards. I called for help after having a really bad day (one of many) at the casino. I don't even remember which casino I was at on that day, Greek Town or Motor City casino, but I do remember being at the lowest point of my entire life.

I am 41 years old, still married, and have two children. I have a 17 year old son, and a 4 year old daughter. I used to drink a lot, but stopped, and without much effort became a compulsive gambler. My life has really turned around since the worst within the last five-plus years. I lost pretty much everything I'd ever worked for. I thank God every day that I sought help, and he saved the only thing that ever meant anything to me, that is my marriage and my family. Five years ago I'd never imagined that I would be in this situation. God bless my wife for hanging in there with me, she has always been there for me. We've been together for 21 years. My compulsive gambling has put me through a great deal of pain, it has taken my self respect, my dignity, and damaged my reputation. In addition to this, my lifetime friendships that I once had have been destroyed, due to the trust that others had in me is now gone. My happiness was taken, my honesty was taken, my life that I once had was taken. Sometimes I feel that I am in a dream/nightmare, and I just want to wake up. I am working hard at getting my life back together, and slowly I am awakening.

Thank you for putting your story out on CD, it has helped me a lot, and has made me realize that we all have issues in life to deal with. Some of these issues are bigger and much greater than others, but we all go through similar experiences. I've replaced the little video clip that's in my head of when I won ten grand on the slot machine, with words off your CD that is "slot machines are for morons!" For some reason I can't forget when you said those words, and I keep thinking of that when I get urges. Thanks again, and I'll be waiting for your book.

•   •   •

I'd like to comment on what a wonderful job [in a talk at Cooley Law School, Lansing, Michigan] Mr. Burke did today. My ears were glued to him the entire time because his story is so REAL—it could happen to any one of us. I think it's very beneficial to have him speak more often, and not only in regards to the ethical violations that he's committed, but in regards to how the whole course of his life was changed due to addiction. Many of my colleagues here at Cooley are bordering addiction, and I may perhaps fall victim to it one day, too. Regardless of what the "problem" may be, it IS a problem and will only get bigger without addressing it. His speech showed me that no matter how good YOU believe things to be going, they may be spiraling out of control. Thank you for allowing him to come here and speak to us and warn us of the situations that may arise in our careers. I hope we get a chance to have him come back to Cooley.

•   •   •

Michael,

I want to thank you for taking the time and speaking with our class this evening. It was hands down the best experience I have had in the UDM [University of Detroit–Mercy] addictions experience. I hope that we will be able to continue discussing this and other addictions. Your willingness to share your experiences is priceless to a student like me.

• • •

I am not a gambler and don't even know one game from another. But the speech is informative and very moving—useful to us other addicts who might not otherwise understand either our own addiction(s) as well, or the nature of gambling addiction. Great work. Sorry for the price you are paying.

• • •

Excellent presentation. . . . .It is so important to hear stories and the logical progression of any addiction: misery.

• • •

AWESOME; very insightful. Never would have expected a person so successful and respected to develop a problem of such severity.

• • •

I thought his speech was awesome. I appreciate it greatly. It warns me that I may be susceptible to a gambling addiction. I don't like it that much but I do have an addictive personality.

• • •

I thought this speech was very interesting. I learned that gambling and alcohol kind of go hand-in-hand and how easy it would be for me to become addicted to gambling with my addictive behavior with alcohol.

• • •

I quit drinking and found that my gambling increased during that period.

⋅ ⋅ ⋅

I truly appreciate the depth of your openness and honesty. Through your experience and courage, you will help so many people. You have inspired me to be brave and follow through with my second recovery and use my story to help others.

⋅ ⋅ ⋅

Great talk. I never would have thought to watch out for this. I wish you the best of luck.

⋅ ⋅ ⋅

Mike—I came from the casino straight here, and I love slot machines. Got third drunk driving on the way back from the casino. Need advice. . . .

⋅ ⋅ ⋅

I really found your testimony very inspiring. You're a very courageous man with an addictive behavior yet a huge heart and soul. God only isolated you to get you to call upon Him once again. So with or without being addicted, don't push Him away. You're loved and blessed. You show it with tremendous heart. I know I've been addicted to drugs, but because of you, I'll never gamble, and damn—I just came of age!

⋅ ⋅ ⋅

Very inspirational speaker. His current dignity and self-respect after his experiences show that we, too, can regain our self-respect and start a new life. Thank you for the warning! I will never gamble.

⋅ ⋅ ⋅

Very moving, riveting, and educational speech. God bless you!

⋅ ⋅ ⋅

Very informative and eye-opening to see the correlation between alcoholism and gambling. My mother, aunt, and their parents are compulsive gamblers. Thanks for the talk.

⋅ ⋅ ⋅

I have seen Michael Burke speak on two occasions. While his talk has a humorous tone at times, he's addressing a very real issue. The consequences he faced as a result of his addiction are fairly typical ones. The life of an addict is never glamorous. It doesn't matter whether the addiction is alcohol, gambling, drugs, crime, sex, food, shopping, television etc. The life of an addict is always the same. There is no excitement, no glamour and no fun. There are no good times. There is no happiness. There is no future and there is no escape. The only solution to take it one day at a time and to always do the next right thing. As long as an alcoholic doesn't pick up that first drink, he can't get drunk. A drug addict can't get high if he just doesn't take the first drug of choice.

It's really very simple, yet it is one of the hardest concepts to hold onto.

Appendix B
Letters to the Court

Gambling has a tremendous impact on communities. The obvious problems are the financial ones. Compulsive gamblers lose their homes, invade their retirement accounts, and force their families into bankruptcies. Most of this is not discussed publicly because the gambler and his or her family are too humiliated to share with their neighbors the true reasons for their financial problems.

Communities also suffer personal losses when individuals who had been involved in leadership roles in the community acknowledge that they have a gambling problem. The loss that is felt is in many ways worse than a death. The sense of betrayal is overpowering.

I had been a leader in the small community of Howell for 25 years. On the day I turned myself in, shock waves reverberated around the city. People who knew me refused to believe the story was true. One person told me that after he heard the news, that night he called his family together for a family meeting so he could tell them. He said that his children cried. They were friends of my daughters.

At the time of my sentencing, community members volunteered to write letters of support to the court. Excerpts from some of those letters follow.

•   •   •

June 6, 2001
Dear Judge Collette:
I understand Mike Burke's sentencing is coming up soon. As a citizen of Howell, I am writing to ask for your leniency while considering his sentence.

My husband has had an optometric practice in Howell for 29 years. I recently closed a gift shop in downtown Howell that I successfully ran for eight years. We have four children ages 17 to 34 years and are proud grandparents of seven. I am including this background information so you can better understand with our businesses and family we have strong roots in this community. It is my belief that Jane and Mike Burke share the same strong roots. Mike's numerous contributions to our schools, his clients, his friends, and especially his family, explain the grief our town felt when news of his crime was made public. Along with feelings of disbelief, was a sense of mourning throughout our town. During the past several weeks, my family and I have not heard one person say a derogatory remark against Mike. Instead, comments such as "he is such a pillar of this community," "I feel like my best friend just died," "the schools are going to be at a loss," "his wife and kids are wonderful," etc., are all being expressed everywhere you go in town.

Having had several conversations about Mike's situation with a diversified group of people, I feel compelled to ask you to consider this man's attributes and to see this crime as a consequence of an addiction. I am not saying that what he did was right or acceptable, but, as with all addictions, the true character of the person is being controlled. I feel by sending him to prison will only serve to take a beaten man down further.

Mike's past record in this community stands for itself. Mike being sent to prison is akin to medieval times where a person was sent to debtors' prison until he could make restitution for his crime . . . and of course, he never could. Justice, in my opinion, would be better served by allowing him to be rehabilitated for his addiction, so he can become healthy again and able to pay restitution to the families that were violated.

Please consider allowing our community to continue to benefit from Mike's support.

Sincerely,

Sandee Greene

• • •

June 1, 2001

Dear Judge Collette:

I am writing this letter in support of Mr. Michael Burke who is scheduled to appear before you on June 18, 2001. While I am aware that Mr. Burke has pled guilty to some very serious infractions, I do not believe that a severe punishment is appropriate in this particular case. I feel that Mr. Burke's circumstances warrant an in-depth, empathetic evaluation considering the pain and suffering currently being experienced by the entire Burke family.

I am certain you would agree that there is a major difference between criminal activity that is harmful to other persons from that which results from personality anomalies. While Mr. Burke might be guilty of human frailty, he is also an extremely involved and highly valued member of our community who has served his "family" tirelessly and with great affection.

This "family" extends beyond wife and children. It includes an extended community family, particularly the Howell Public School community.

I have worked with Mr. Burke on many occasions with regard to school issues and bond fund-raising elections. He has always demonstrated the highest levels of interest, energy, and caring. He has repeatedly extended his physical, financial, and spiritual support every time it was requested. In this day and age, to find a person who wishes to actively participate in improving the quality of life of so many others is, indeed, rare.

As you arrive at your decision, I sincerely hope that you will consider the views of myself and the many others as we speak out in support of Mr. Burke and the many

*valued contributions he has made to our community. I trust
that you will be deliberate in your ruling, but I hope com-
passionate to a most valued member of our community.*
Sincerely,
Sue Swartz, Vice President
Howell Public Schools Board of Education

• • •

June 2001
Dear Sir:

*I am writing you in regards to the upcoming sentenc-
ing of Michael Burke regarding his crime of embezzlement.*

*My family and I have known Mike for many years. We
became acquainted through our children and school.
When the news of Mike's indiscretion was about to be
made public, in an act I can only call unbelievably brave,
his younger daughter Katey told her closest friends. She
wanted them to hear it first-hand and not on the news or
in the paper. When my daughter Tiffany told me that evening, we both wept for the family and for Mike himself. I
was in total shock because knowing this man and his family for so long, it seemed like a nightmare, not anything
near real.*

*This is a man who never missed an event that his
daughters were participating in, a man who together with
his high school sweetheart and now devoted wife opened
their home so often to kids for pool parties, float decorat-
ing, pompon garage sales, and a host of other things. I
guess you would call them the All-American Family. I
truly believe that they would do anything for the people
they cared about and for their family.*

*After the shock of what my daughter told me eased
up, my prayers turned to Jane, Katey, Amy, and then to
Mike himself. I felt for his family and for the families that
were affected by his crime, but I have to be honest and say
that my heart broke for Mike as well. Knowing how much*

he loves his family, friends, and community, I knew he must have been in pain for so long keeping this terrible secret. The thought of knowing how it would affect the people he held so dear and the life that he worked so hard to build in the community he loves had to torment him. I think a weaker person might have taken an easy yet tragic way out.

I believe that good people do bad things and addictions can overtake your life to the point that you don't even recognize your own self in the mirror. I know this first-hand because my father, I am proud and thankful to say, is a recovering alcoholic for the past 30 years. I remember in his drinking days the difference between a sober dad and a drunk dad. The two were totally different people. Coupled with his drinking addiction he also liked to gamble. Two evils, but underneath one incredibly fine man. I recall it taking over his life and our lives to the point of an almost final destruction. Then by the grace of God he admitted himself to the hospital and got the treatment he so desperately needed. I remember back then thinking that my dad is not a bad guy; he is sick and he needs help. My family believed in him, just like the Burkes believe in Mike. They know what he did was wrong, but also know the kind of father, husband, and friend he has been all these years and stand by him accordingly.

I find it amazing and heartwarming that upon the news of this tragedy, I did not hear anyone who really knows Mike say one thing bad about him. All the responses were the same—shock, sadness, support, prayer, and more prayer. My daughter and I were on choir tour in the thick of all this, and together as a group we held hands and prayed for the family and for Mike. Not just me, not just my daughter, but a choir of people! People who know that bad things happen to good people and not to pass judgment because addictions can happen to anyone. Anyone.

It is my hope that when you decide the fate of Mike and ultimately his family that you look at the man, not just the crime. That you take into consideration the soul of the person, not the addiction that has recently taken hold of his life. Just like a person with diabetes, depression, or even cancer, addictions are a sickness that with help can be treated and overcome.

I thank God every time I am with my father and family that we were given the chance to see him at his full potential and experience all he has to offer. His experiences in life have given others the knowledge and determination to beat their addictions including one of his very best friends and former drinking buddies. So in a sense I guess you could say he has been a teacher and out of something bad came some good. Knowing the kind of man Mike is, I truly believe that he too can become a teacher, a success story. There are so many bad people in the world, but Mike Burke isn't one of them. Yes, he should have to make restitution and yes he needs to get treatment, but going to jail would be even a bigger crime than the one he committed. He doesn't belong there; many do; he doesn't. Let him pay back his debt, let him be a teacher to others, make use of all he has to offer, give him the chance to prove to you, his family, and mostly himself that he is still the good man that he always has been.

I pray that these words will not fall on deaf ears and that you will truly consider all that is at stake during your difficult decision.

Sincerely,

Darla Maroudis and Family

• • •

June 7, 2001

Dear Judge Collette,

It is unfortunate that I am writing this letter to you because I know that the sentencing for embezzlement is awaiting Mike Burke. I must take the opportunity to make a plea to you for leniency when determining the sentence for Mr. Burke. No doubt, he is not denying his part in the crime, nor am I suggesting that there is no sentence. In many ways, Mike has jeopardized the loss of his career, tarnished the high level of respect in his community of peers, and been responsible on the unfathomable amount of stress and grief he has brought to his wife and children. I know you will let justice prevail.

However, I must share with you that I was a middle-school teacher in Howell and presently holding the position as an assistant principal at the high school. Throughout the past ten years, I have seen Mr. Burke in the community. He always attends school functions and is there supporting not only his daughters, but also the other students. He has shown his support for school and community elections.

More recently, he handled a divorce for me. I was filing for a divorce and was frightened that I would be left in financial ruin. He was very comforting, reassuring, and only charged me a thousand dollars because he said, "You are a teacher in the community, you give back every day, and public school employees aren't paid what they're worth."

I know that being a kind person doesn't excuse criminal behavior, but I do know that gambling is an addiction no different than alcoholism. I lost a father to alcoholism when he was only 44. Not because he didn't know that alcoholism would kill him, but because he couldn't control it. That was in 1970.

Fortunately in 2001, the medical and psychology professions understand more about addictive behaviors. I truly believe that in spite of understanding the law and the consequences for breaking the law, Mike Burke couldn't control his addiction. My hope is that Mike is able to face his current situation and have this be a life-changing event. I am confident that he will face these

charges, sentence, and addiction with the same dedica-
tion and integrity that he has shown our community in the
past.
Respectfully,
Margaret M. Drotar

• • •

June 5, 2001
The Honorable William E. Collette:

I am writing on behalf of Mr. Michael Burke and the
sentencing aspect for his admission of the crime of em-
bezzlement which comes before you on June 18, 2001. I
have known Michael since I arrived in Howell in the
spring of 1988. He was the attorney for the sellers of the
home which we purchased. A problem developed with the
title of the property and we dealt with Michael on that
problem for the next six months. He performed admirably
and with dispatch within the framework established by
the law.

Fortunately, I had many more experiences with
Michael in my professional capacity of Superintendent of
Howell Public Schools for the period of nine years, be-
ginning in June, 1988 through June, 1997. Michael was
very visible in the community, participating both as a fa-
ther with school activities as well as offering his expertise
as an attorney and mediator. He was a significant partic-
ipant as a member of a citizens' group selected by both
the Board of Education of Howell and the Howell Teach-
ers Union to mediate a stalemate in contract negotiations
between the two parties. Michael offered a voice of rea-
son and conciliation which was valued by the two parties
and the other community leaders participating in this
process. As a result of this intervention, a strike was
averted.

On several other occasions, Michael was an active
participant in the citizens committee which volunteered
to campaign for the passage of school bond issues and

mileage campaigns. Michael would speak to parent and civic groups, giving freely of his time on behalf of his family and his community. I was always impressed by the respect he received during these meetings, a quality I attributed to his sincerity and his reputation for fairness. I was also aware that when Michael committed himself to a project such as this, he stayed with it to the end and followed through on his commitment.

Please accept these comments on behalf of Michael as an indication of my faith in his being a valued member of the Howell community and worthy of your consideration for inpatient treatment for his addiction rather than lengthy incarceration. I would hope that through this treatment he would return to being a contributing member of our community and society in general. Michael has already demonstrated his character by admitting his guilt and requesting consideration for treatment of his addiction. Given this course of action, he could ultimately return to the work force and make restitution for his debts.

Thank you for giving me the opportunity to make a plea on Michael's behalf.
Very truly yours,
Charles W. Manuel, PhD
Superintendent, Retired, Howell Public Schools

• • •

The Honorable William E. Collette,

As an eighth grade teacher with 32 years experience, I meet thousands of parents. I am writing to you on behalf of Mike Burke. He is one of the finest parents with whom I have ever had the opportunity to work.

I must smile whenever I think of Mike in relationship to his daughters. Years before I had Katey in class, I noted Mike and Jane at many of her functions, as well as with their oldest daughter, Amy, who attended Highlander Way Middle School. I observed their interaction at local dance recitals and at the McDonald's and Optimist Club county-wide speech contests and Odyssey of the Mind regional tournaments. I remember thinking at that time how nice it would be to have Katey in my class at McPherson Middle School.

I truly admire every single aspect of Mike's life of which I am aware. He was extraordinarily helpful during the only teacher strike in which I was ever involved, leading the settlement so both sides were happy and the community felt they won. He has helped people I have recommended to him for his services, lowering fees to match their needs.

Mostly, however, I know Mike as a parent. I would not see Michael Burke judged harshly because his nature is never to judge others at all. I would hope you will weigh all of the good he has done by building a solid family structure for children and a wife who never have to guess how deeply they are loved. I would hope you would weigh all of the good he has done a growing community of people who never have enough kindness shown them by others who care. Mike Burke has touched my life. I wrote an unsolicited letter of similar nature to Katey after I read of this situation and am moved to write to you for clemency on his behalf. People with addictive personalities need therapy, not cold consequences.

It's time to give back to Mike Burke.

Sincerely,

Kathy Rubin, Howell Public Schools

•   •   •

June 10, 2001

To: The Honorable William E. Collette,

I am writing a letter regarding the upcoming sentencing of Michael J. Burke.

Having had the privilege of knowing Michael for the past twenty years, I can look back in pride to his outstanding community leadership and incredible devotion to his wife and two children. It has been my pleasure to meet with Mike on both personal and business matters and watch him "set the pace" for community leadership and the great support of his children in all their school activities.

It is most regretful that Mike has fallen into such an insidious addiction as that of gambling. An addiction which robs one of independence, dignity, and finally, choice. I know this episode has been devastating to both Mike and his family, though their continued love and support of each other has been gratifying to watch.

I would ask the court to take into consideration all that Mike has done for our schools and community over the years. The support he has from his family and many friends and most importantly the support he can receive from the outstanding addiction programs in our region.

I wish Michael and his family the very best for a full recovery and a bright future. Thank you for allowing me to express my hopes for Michael and his family.
Sincerely,
Ronald G. Hughes

• • •

Dear Judge Collette,

My family and I have known Michael for many years. I was born on his ninth birthday and he was our paperboy as I grew up. He was a good friend of my oldest brother back as playing high school football together and the friendship remains strong today. He is like a brother to me, without the sibling "stuff," and like one of their kids to my parents.

Now here we are on what one might assume to be the other side of Michael's legal problems. He has hurt and betrayed us by taking our money. Money that would have been willingly given to our friend had he simply asked for our help. Was it taken by the man that we know, trust, and love? The answer is complicated because we firmly believe that Michael, while in the grips of the disease of addiction, gambled the money away.

Would the Michael we have all known and loved merely cheated us for his own gain were he not an addict? We say no, not in a lifetime. Would he intentionally hurt any of us just to hurt us? Not the Michael we know. We are sure there are some who wonder if we know who Michael really is and we are certain that we do. He's the man that would stand up for the underdog, look out for the people he cares about and work to leave the world a better place because he was in it.

This is a man who would say yes to a favor, before he knew what was being asked. In fact there were many occasions through the years that Michael spent time willingly to offer sound legal advice. In addition, since Michael's alcohol recovery, he has been very active in helping those working toward their own sobriety. Time and compassion has never been a shortage if anyone asked for Michael's help. That is the kind of man and friend he is to others and to us.

Would we have Michael represent us legally in the future if we could? Absolutely. It is our opinion that he has an excellent legal mind and has profoundly represented many, in addition to us, over the years. Is gambling less addictive than cigarettes or alcohol? Absolutely not. In fact, there are experts who believe it to be an addiction stronger than that of heroin. Some have gone on to say that gambling is three times harder than heroin to kick.

The question is how does society punish someone who committed betrayal and crime as a result of an addiction? Yes, there has to be punishment, but what good would sending Michael to jail serve? Will it return monies to my parents, to others, or to me? No. Would it cure Michael of his addiction? No. Would it serve society in any real way? We do NOT believe so. Would it act as a deterrent to others? We have our serious doubts.

However, we do ask that you not send Michael where he can be of no use to anyone. Our hurt would be less-

ened if he is allowed to get the treatment of his disease he needs and if he is allowed to begin again. He has much to give back to his community if he is allowed to do so. Load him up with community service! Let him be an example to others in a way that will help someone else before they are also consumed by a disease that is little understood and that can damage the lives of family and friends.

It is our sincerest hope that Michael will be allowed to serve his community by perhaps spending time educating people, young adults especially, about the devastation that unchecked, untreated cross-addiction can cause. We are certain that his own opinion and punishment of himself is greater than anything anyone can impose.

Thank you for the court's time.
Sincerely,
Phyllis J. Reid, Bob Reid, Jean Reid

[The Reids are all victims of my embezzlement.]

Appendix C
Lawyer Assistance Programs

ALABAMA

Lawyer Assistance Program
http://www.alabar.org/
    brochures/alap-addiction.pdf
334-834-7576
E-mail: jeannemarie.leslie@
    alabar.org

ALASKA

Lawyers Assistance Committee
907-264-0401
E-mail: oregand@alaskabar
    .org

ARIZONA

Member Assistance Program
http://www.myazbar.org/
    Members/map.cfm
602-340-7313
Crisis Line 800-681-3057
    24 hours
E-mail: hal.nevitt@staff
    .azbar.org

ARKANSAS

Arkansas Lawyers Assistance
    Program (ArJLAP)
http://www.arlap.org/

501-907-2529
E-mail: confidential@arjlap.org

CALIFORNIA

State Bar of California LAP
http://calbar.ca.gov/lap
Toll-free 877-LAP 4 HELP
E-mail: Richard.Carlton@calbar
    .ca.gov

The Other Bar
http://www.otherbar.org/
415-482-9500
800-222-0767
E-mail: resner2100@comcast
    .net

COLORADO

Colorado Lawyer's Health
    Program
http://www.clhp.org/
800-432-0977 or
303-832-2233
E-mail: confidential@clhp
    .org

Colorado Attorney Assistance
    Program (CAAP)
http://www
    .minesandassociates.com/

A voluntary & confidential program sponsored by the Colorado Supreme Court, available 24/7/365
800-873-7138 or
303-832-1068

CONNECTICUT

Lawyers Concerned for Lawyers
http://www.lclct.org/
860-563-4900
E-mail: info@lclct.org

DELAWARE

Delaware Lawyers Assistance Program (DE-LAP)
http://www.abanet.org/
 legalservices/colap/www
 .DE-LAP.org
Carol P. Waldhauser, Executive Director
301 N. Market Street
Wilmington, DE 19801
Phone: 302-777-0124 or
 1-877-24DELAP
Fax: 302-658-5212
E-mail: cwaldhauser@de-lap
 .org

DISTRICT OF COLUMBIA

Lawyer Counseling Program
http://www.dcbar.org/for
 _lawyers/bar_services/
 counseling/index.cfm
202-347-3131 9:00 - 5:00 and answering machine
E-mail: lphillips@dcbar.org

FLORIDA

Florida Lawyers Assistance, Inc.
http://www.fla-lap.org/
800-282-8981 (National)
 24 hours
E-mail: mail@fla-lap.org

GEORGIA

Drug & Alcohol Resource Center
800-327-9631
E-mail:
 dwfjr@theresourcecenter.org

HAWAII

Hawaii Supreme Court Attorneys and Judges Assistance Program
http://www.hawaiiaap.com/
Steve Dixon, JD, Executive Director
801 Alakea St., Ste. 209
Honolulu, Hi. 96813
(808) 531-2880
E-mail: sdixon@interpac.net
Attorney & Judges Assistance Program
808-531-2880 24 hours
E-mail: goddess1@lavanet.com

IDAHO

Idaho Lawyer Assistance Program
http://www2.state.id.us/isb/
 gen/lap.htm
208-334-4500

E-mail:
LAP@southworthassociates
.net

ILLINOIS

Lawyers' Assistance Program,
Inc.
http://www.illinoislap.org/
index.html
Chicago Office: 312-726-6607
or 800-LAP-1233
Downstate Office: 618-462-
4397 or 800-LAP-1233
Chicago E-mail:
jpvoss@illinoislap.org
Downstate E-mail:
jbartylak@illinoislap.org

INDIANA

Judges and Lawyers
Assistance Program
http://www.in.gov/judiciary/
ijlap/
866-428-5527 (JLAP) or
317-833-0370
E-mail:
tharrell@courts.state.in.us

IOWA

Lawyers Helping Lawyers
800-243-1533
E-mail: hughgrady@mac
.com

KANSAS

Impaired Lawyers Assistance
Committee

888-342-9080
E-mail: help@kalap.com

KENTUCKY

Kentucky Lawyers Assistance
Program (KYLAP)
http://www.kybar.org/persprof
.htm
502-545-1801 Cell
(Confidential)
502-607-0424 Home
502-564-3225 Fax
502-564-3795, ext. 265 KBA
E-mail: hebert@kybar.org

LOUISIANA

Alcohol & Drug Abuse
Committee
866-354-9334 24 hours
E-mail: louisianalap@worldnet
.att.net

MAINE

Maine Assistance Program for
Lawyers
1-800-530-4627
E-mail:
maineasstprog@verizon.net

MARYLAND

Lawyer Assistance Program
http://www.msba.org/sec
_comm/committees/
lawyerassist/index.htm
410-685-7878 Ext. 3040 &
3041 24 hours
800-492-1964

E-mail 1: rvincent@msba.org
or E-mail 2:
cwaldhauser@msba.org

MASSACHUSETTS

Lawyers Concerned for
Lawyers, Inc.
http://www.lclma.org/
617-482-9600 or
800-525-0210
E-mail: email@lclma.org

MICHIGAN

Lawyers & Judges Assistance
Program
http://www.michbar.org/
generalinfo/ljap/
517-346-6306
800-996-5522
E-mail:
mburkett@mail.michbar
.org

MINNESOTA

Lawyers Concerned for
Lawyers
http://mnlcl.org/
651-646-5590
E-mail: help@mnlcl.org

MISSISSIPPI

Lawyers and Judges
Assistance Program
http://www.msbar.org/lawyers
_assist.php
800-593-9777
24 hour confidential hotline

E-mail:
bdaugherty@msbar.org

MISSOURI

Lawyers' Assistance
Program
http://mobar.org/law/achabu
.shtml
800-688-7859 24 hours &
answering service
573-638-2262
E-mail: jbrady@mobar.org

MONTANA

Lawyers Helping Lawyers
Carol Frazer - Coordinator
535 Saddle Drive
Helena, MT 59601
Phone: 888-385-9119 or
406-439-0055
Fax: 406/449-8828

NEBRASKA

Alcohol & Drug Abuse
Committee
http://www.nebar.com/
memberinfo/services/nlap
.htmhttp://www.nebar.com/
memberinfo/services/nlap
.htm
402-475-6527
E-mail: rallan@nebar.com

NEVADA

Lawyers Concerned for
Lawyers
702-455-4827

E-mail: GRAHAMR@co.clark
.nv.us

NEW HAMPSHIRE

New Hampshire Lawyers
Assistance Program
Hotline 877-224-6060 (24/7)
E-mail: cecieh@lapnh.org

NEW JERSEY

Lawyers Assistance Program
http://www.njlap.com/
800-246-5527 24 hours
E-mail: njlap@aol.com

NEW MEXICO

Lawyers' Assistance Program
505-242-6845
505-228-1948 local helpline
(24-hr)
800-860-4914 statewide
helpline (24-hr)
E-mail jyeag@unm.edu

NEW YORK

Lawyers Helping Lawyers
http://www.nysba.org/Content/
NavigationMenu/Attorney
_Resources/Lawyer
_Assistance_Program
_(LAP)/Lawyer_Assistance
Program(LAP).htm
800-255-0569 24 hours
(Nationwide)
E-mail: lap@nysba.org
Nassau County Bar
Association LAP

http://www.nassaubar.org/
lawyers_assistance_program
.cfm
516-747-4070
888-408-6222
E-mail: peter@nassaubar.org

LAP related resource in New
York
New York Lawyer Assistance
Trust
http://www.nylat.org/
518-285-4545

New York City

New York City Lawyer
Assistance Program
Enter this website, http://www
.abcny.org/
click onto the LAWYER
ASSISTANCE PROGRAM
box to enter NYC LAP
212-302-5787 24 Hours
E-mail: etravis@abcny.org

NORTH CAROLINA

BarCARES of North Carolina
http://www.ncbar.org/public/
barCARES/index.aspx
1-800-640-0735
E-mail: hrcch@aol.com or
E-mail: cclcooper@cs.com

North Carolina Lawyer
Assistance Program
http://www.nclap.org/
800-720-7257
E-mail: nclap@bellsouth.net

NORTH DAKOTA

State Bar of North Dakota
701-255-1404

OHIO

Ohio Lawyers Assistance
 Program, Inc.
http://www.ohiolap.org/
800-348-4343 24 hours
E-mail: smote@ohiolap.org

OKLAHOMA

Lawyers Helping Lawyers
800-364-7886
E-mail:
 mirandolaw@dellnet.com

OREGON

Oregon Attorney Assistance
 Program
http://www.oaap.org/
503-226-1057
E-mail: ShariG@oaap.org

PENNSYLVANIA

Lawyers Concerned for
 Lawyers Helpline
888-999-1941
Office Number 800-335-2572
E-mail: ken@lclpa.org

RHODE ISLAND

Confidential Assistance
 Program
401-421-5740
E-mail: hmcdonald@ribar.com

SOUTH CAROLINA

Lawyers Helping Lawyers
866-545-9590
E-mail:
 robert.turnbull@scbar.org

SOUTH DAKOTA

Lawyers Concerned for
 Lawyers
605-624-4449
E-mail: mccahren@iw.net

TENNESSEE

Tennessee Lawyers Assistance
 Program
http://www.tlap.org/
877-424-8527
E-mail: tnlap@aol.com

TEXAS

Texas Lawyers Assistance
 Program
http://www.texasbar.com/
 members/buildpractice/tlap/
 tlap.asp
800-343-8527
Voice Mail 512-463-1453
E-mail: afoster@texasbar.com

UTAH

Lawyers Helping Lawyers
http://www
 .lawyershelpinglawyers.org/
 pages/350744/index.htm
Local Phone: 801-579-0404
Toll Free: 800-530-3743

E-mail:
sjohnson@lawyershelpingla
wyers.org

VERMONT

Lawyer Assistance Program
http://www.vtbar.org/mbrben
.htm#lawyerassistance
802-773-9109 ext. 21
E-mail: barclayone@aol.com

VIRGINIA

Lawyers Helping Lawyers
http://www.valhl.org/
877-LHL-INVA
(877-545-4682) Confidential
Voice Mail 804-644-3212
E-mail: info@valhl.org

WASHINGTON

Lawyers Assistance Program
http://www.wsba.org/lasd/lasd
-lap.html
206-727-8265
E-mail: barbarah@wsba.org

WEST VIRGINIA

Lawyer Committee on
Assistance and Intervention
304-231-0441
E-mail: karen.kahle@
steptoe-johnson.com

WISCONSIN

Lawyers Assistance Program
http://www.wisbar.org/wislap/
800-543-2625 (24/7 helpline)

E-mail: chayne@wisbar.org

WYOMING

Lawyers Assistance
Committee
307-778-7663

PUERTO RICO

Committee for Lawyer Affairs
809-751-2705

VIRGIN ISLANDS

Lawyer Assistance Committee
340-773-4150
E-mail: lmingus@viaccess.net

CANADA

Alberta Lawyers Assist
Program
http://www
.albertalawyersassist.ca/
Professional Help: 1-800–461-
8908 or (403) 237-8880
Executive Director 1-877-737-
5508 or (403) 537-5508
E-mail: alap@nucleus.com

British Columbia Lawyers
Assistance Program
http://www.lapbc.com/
604-685-2171 or 888-685-2171
E-mail: derek@lapbc.com

Legal Profession Assistance
Conference of the Canadian
Bar Association (LPAC)
http://www.lpac.ca/
800-667-5722
E-mail: joyces@cba.org

Ontario Lawyers' Assistance
  Program
http://www.olap.ca/
Leota Embleton, Program
  Manager
5025 Orbitor Drive, Bldg. 2,
  Suite 220
Mississauga ON L4W 4Y5
Local Phone: (905) 238-1740
Toll Free: (877) 576-6227
Fax: (905) 238-1740
E-mail: leota@olap.ca

Quebec Bar Association
PAMBA Lawyers Association
514-286-0831
E-mail:
  guyquesnel@videotran.ca

**ENGLAND/WALES/
SCOTLAND**

LawCare
011-44-1273 461861
E-mail.hilary@lawcare.org
  .uk

Index